The Creative Curriculum® *for* Preschool

Teaching Guide

featuring the Simple Machines Study

Erin Seagraves and Heather Baker

 **Teaching**Strategies® · Bethesda, MD

Copyright © 2016 by Teaching Strategies, LLC.

All rights reserved. No part of this text may be reproduced in any form or by any electronic or mechanical means, including information storage and retrieval systems, without prior written permission from Teaching Strategies, LLC, except in the case of brief quotations embodied in critical articles or reviews.

An exception is also made for the forms and the letters to families that are included in this guide. Permission is granted to duplicate those pages for use by the teachers/providers of the particular program that purchased these materials in order to implement *The Creative Curriculum® for Preschool* in the program. However, the material on those pages may not be duplicated for training purposes without the express written permission of Teaching Strategies, LLC.

The publisher and the authors cannot be held responsible for injury, mishap, or damages incurred during the use of or because of the information in this book. The authors recommend appropriate and reasonable supervision at all times based on the age and capability of each child. It is advisable teachers not distribute photos of children or post them online without written consent from parents or guardians. Photos and videos should be kept internally absent written consent from parents or guardians.

English editing: Kimberly Maxwell, Dana Wood
Design and layout: Jeff Cross, Jennifer Love King, Abner Nieves
Spanish translation: Rosi Perea
Cover design: Abner Nieves

Teaching Strategies, LLC
Bethesda, MD 20814

www.TeachingStrategies.com

978-1-60617-697-9

Library of Congress Control Number: 2015959013

Teaching Strategies, The Creative Curriculum, Mighty Minutes, Mega Minutos, and the open book/open door logo are registered trademarks of Teaching Strategies, LLC, Bethesda, MD. Brand-name products of other companies are suggested for illustrative purposes and are not required for implementation of the curriculum.

2 3 4 5 6 7 8 9 10 11   22 21 20 19 18 17
    Printing   Year Printed

Printed and bound in China.

Table of Contents

Getting Started

Why Investigate Simple Machines?

Simple machines are all around us. The slide on the playground, the scissors in the Art area, and the cap on the water bottle are all examples of the simple machines in children's lives. Children are in constant contact with so many different types of simple machines!

What makes this study engaging is that there are many everyday opportunities for children to interact with simple machines such as ramps, screws, and levers. In the Art area, they use scissors, hole punchers, and staplers to create and explore art concepts; on the playground they use wheelbarrows to carry around loads of toys and enjoy going down the slide; and while cooking and preparing foods, they use tongs, knives, and forks. In almost every area of the classroom, children have opportunities to use simple machines.

A study of simple machines helps children to learn about the characteristics that make up the six different types of simple machines. Using these characteristics, they can identify simple machines around their homes, outdoors, and in the classroom. They will learn how simple machines are used for different types of work and play and see how simple machines are combined to make complex machines. When children work together to create their own simple machines, they use a variety of skills to plan, write, draw, build, and negotiate with others.

In this study, children will investigate how each type of simple machine helps make work easier. They will investigate how inclined planes help move things, how levers are used, and how screws hold things together. Children will learn about other types of simple machines and who works with simple machines. Through these investigations, children will observe forces of nature such as friction and gravity as they slide toys down a ramp. They will experiment with modifying simple machines in different ways, make their own simple machines, and meet interesting people. A study of simple machines also offers a meaningful way for children to use literacy, mathematics, the arts, and science and technology to investigate and represent their understanding of important concepts related to physical development, science, and social studies.

> **How do children in your room show their interest in simple machines? What do they say about the simple machines they use in the classroom?**

Web of Investigations

The Creative Curriculum® for Preschool Teaching Guide, featuring the Simple Machines Study includes five investigations aimed at exploring simple machines. The investigations offer children an opportunity to learn more about the simple machines they use at home and in the classroom as well see how others use simple machines for both work and play.

Some of the investigations include site visits or classroom visits from guest experts who use simple machines every day. Each investigation helps children explore important concepts in science and social studies while strengthening their skills in physical development, literacy, math, technology, and the arts. Expand this web by adding your own ideas, particularly about aspects of the topic that are unique to your community.

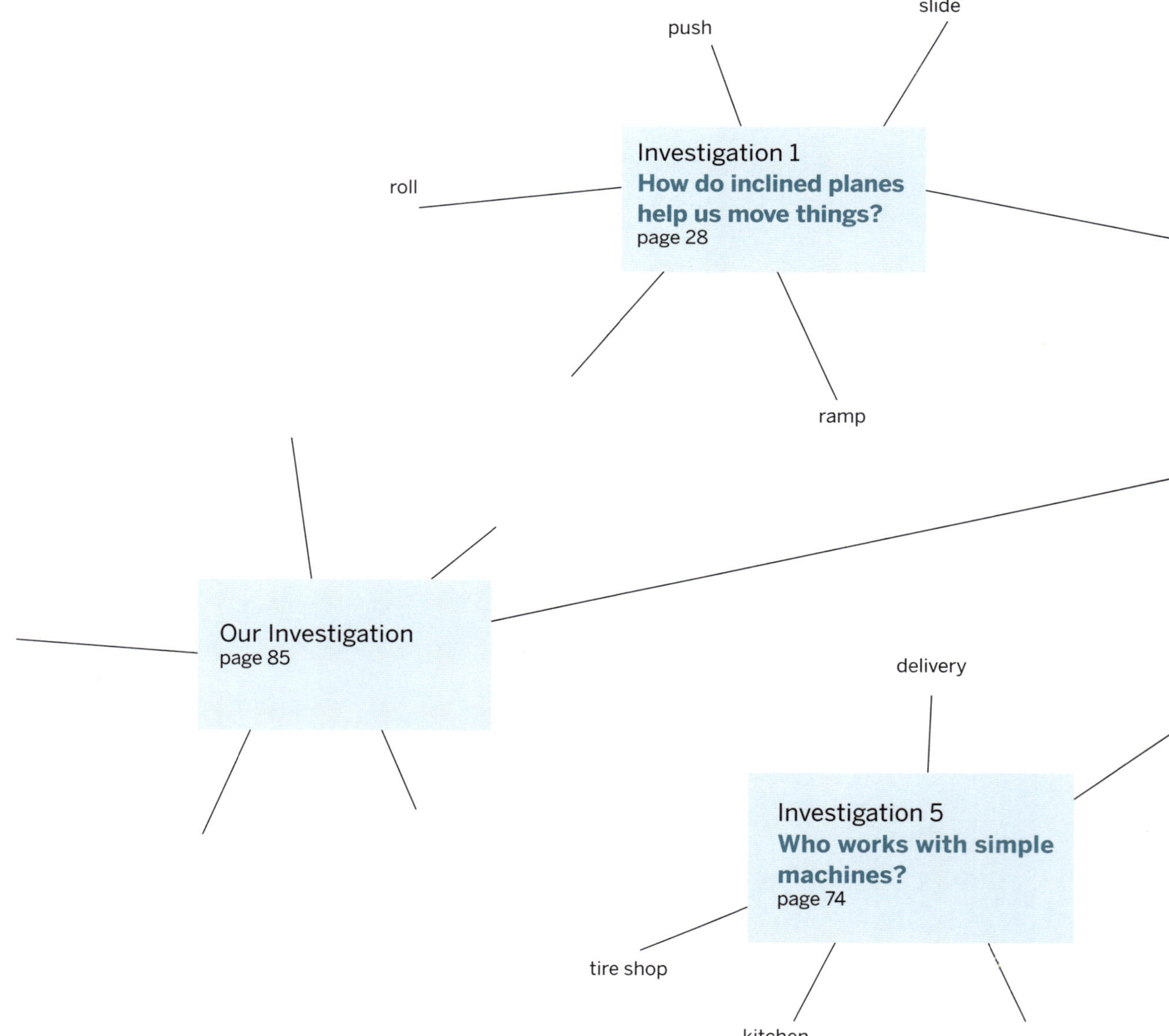

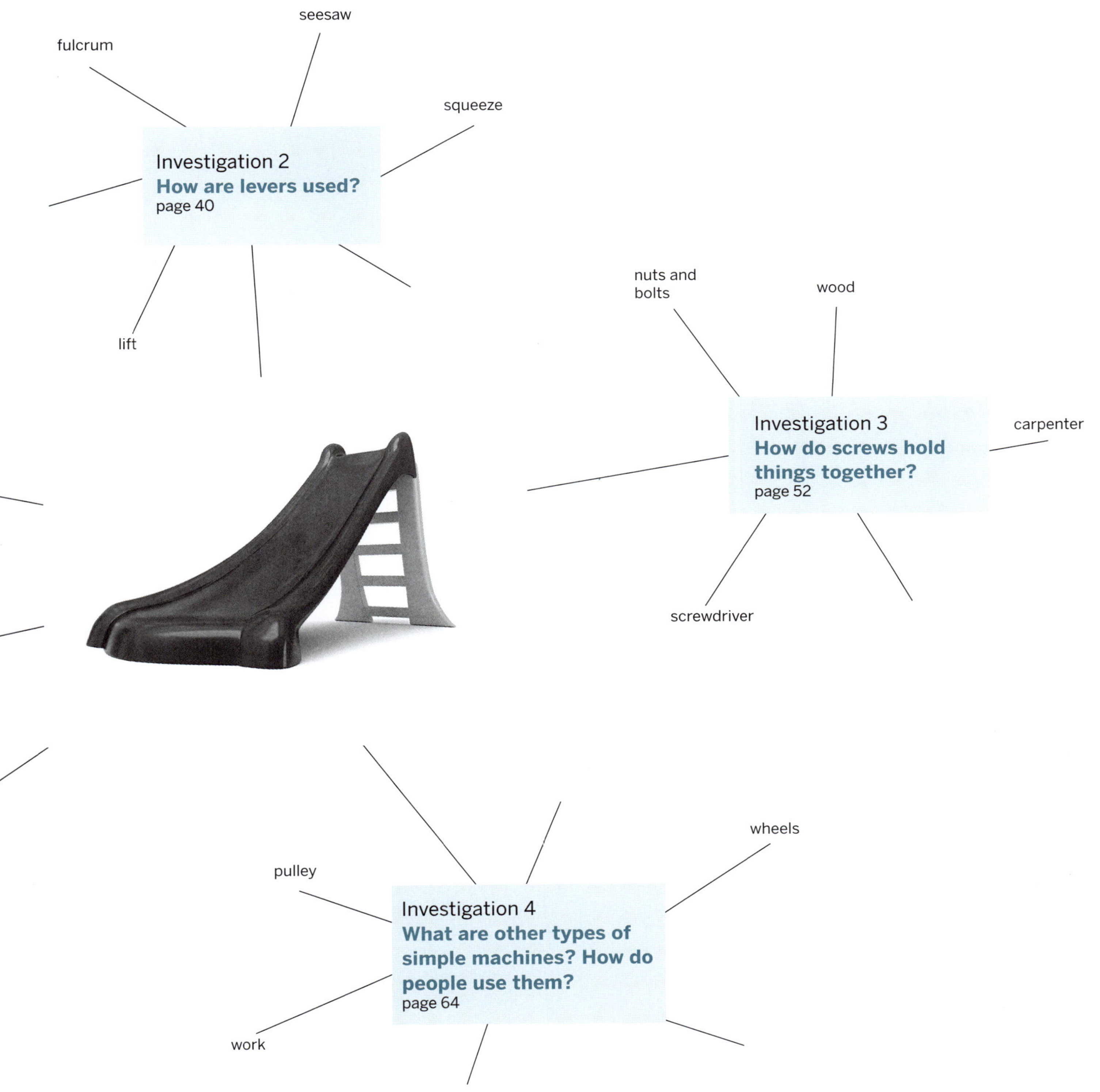
seesaw
fulcrum
squeeze
Investigation 2
How are levers used?
page 40
lift
nuts and
bolts
wood
Investigation 3
How do screws hold
things together?
page 52
carpenter
screwdriver
pulley
wheels
Investigation 4
What are other types of
simple machines? How do
people use them?
page 64
work

A Letter to Families

Send families a letter introducing the study. Use the letter to communicate with families and as an opportunity to invite their participation in the study.

Dear Families,

Preschool children use simple machines as they play and create throughout the day. We have noticed that the children are curious and enjoy experimenting as they use simple machines such as scissors, hole punchers, ramps, slides, and screws. They have shown interest in exploring and modifying simple machines and are curious about how they are used. We think a study of simple machines will be a great opportunity for children to explore their ideas.

We need your help to get our study started. If you can, your help in gathering materials related to simple machines would be valuable in supporting our investigations. We need a variety of materials for the children to explore: tongs, tweezers, lemon presses, and screw-top bottles. If you have any books or pictures related to simple machines, we'd love to borrow those, too. Below is a list of suggested items, but feel free to send other items that would enhance our exploration. Please label your items with your name so we can return them to you at the end of the study. We promise to take good care of them! Also, please let us know if any member of your family works with simple machines (e.g., chef, delivery worker, mover, or carpenter) and would like to share their expertise with the class. We would love to arrange a time for them to join us in our investigations.

Lemon press	Nuts and bolts	Nutcracker
Small boards	Scissors	**Pictures and Videos**
Paper towel tubes	Screws	Interesting simple
Water bottles with caps	Screwdriver	machines
Cardboard	Screwdriver bits	Simple machines being
Corkscrew	Potato ricer	used
Gutter pieces	Jars with lids	Simple machines in
Garlic press	Hole punchers	your home
Chopsticks	Tongs	Simple machines in
Tweezers	Pliers	your community

What You Can Do at Home

Talk with your child about simple machines that you see around your home and neighborhood: screw-top bottles, nuts and bolts, ramps, slides, tongs, tweezers, brooms, etc. Create a list of the simple machines you find. If possible, give your child simple machines that he or she can use and ask questions about how they work. How is the simple machine used? What does it do?

At the end of the study, we will have a special event to show you what we've learned. Thank you for participating in our learning.

Carta a las familias

Envíe una carta a las familias para informarles sobre el estudio. Use la carta para comunicarse y como una oportunidad para invitarles a participar.

Apreciadas familias:

Los niños de preescolar usan máquinas simples mientras juegan y crean durante el día. Hemos notado que los niños son curiosos y disfrutan con la experimentación al usar máquinas simples como las tijeras, perforadoras, rampas, toboganes y tornillos. Han mostrado interés en la exploración y modificación de máquinas simples y en cómo se usan. Pensamos que un estudio sobre las máquinas será una gran oportunidad para que los niños puedan explorar sus ideas.

Para poder realizar nuestro estudio, necesitamos su ayuda para reunir materiales relacionados con máquinas simples, con el fin de investigarlos: pinzas pequeñas, pinzas para cocinar, prensas para limones y botellas con tapa de rosca. Si tienen libros o ilustraciones relacionados con máquinas simples, nos encantaría usarlos. A continuación les ofrecemos algunas sugerencias, pero siéntanse libres de enviar cualquier tipo de artículo que podamos explorar. Por favor, rotulen todos los artículos con sus nombres para poder devolvérselos al final de nuestro estudio. ¡Les prometemos que los cuidaremos bien! Si ustedes o miembros de sus familias trabajan con máquinas simples y les gustaría compartir con el grupo sus conocimientos (e.g., chef, empleado encargado de entregas, empleado de mudanzas o carpintero) por favor déjennos saber. Nos encantaría que participaran en nuestras investigaciones.

Prensa para limones	Tuercas y tornillos	**Ilustraciones y videos**
Tablas pequeñas	Tijeras	
Tubos de papel toalla	Destornillador	Máquinas simples interesantes
Botellas de agua con tapas	Brocas para destornillador	Máquinas simples en uso
Cartón	Majador de papas	Máquinas simples en su hogar
Sacacorcho	Frascos y tapas	
Pedazos de canaleta	Perforadora	Máquinas simples en su comunidad
Prensa para ajos	Pinzas para cocinar	
Palitos chinos	Alicate	
Pinzas pequeñas	Cascanueces	

Qué puede hacer en el hogar

Hable con su niño sobre las máquinas simples que vea en su hogar y en su comunidad: botellas con tapas de rosca, tornillos y tuercas, toboganes, pinzas pequeñas, escobas, etc. Cree una lista de las máquinas simples que encuentren. Si es posible, dele a su niño máquinas simples que él pueda usar y haga preguntas sobre cómo funcionan. ¿Cómo se usa la máquina? ¿Qué hace?

Al finalizar el estudio, tendremos un evento especial para celebrar lo aprendido. Les agradecemos su importante rol en nuestro aprendizaje.

Beginning the Study

Introducing the Topic

To begin this study, you will explore the topic with the children so they can answer the following questions: What do we know about simple machines? What do we want to find out about simple machines?"

A classroom study of simple machines encourages children to experiment with levers, screws, inclined planes, pulleys, wedges, and wheels and axles. It is important to offer materials to make inclined planes, scissors, staplers, balance scales, screws, nuts and bolts, and kitchen utensils such as tongs, forks, and knives. Make sure that the materials you offer are safe for the children. Use children's scissors, butter or plastic knives, and inspect all of the materials to ensure there are no sharp edges that pose a danger to the children. When introducing these materials, it is important to demonstrate how to use them safely and properly.

Begin the study by gathering many different types of simple machines that you will investigate throughout the study. Also collect pictures and photos for your collection. Look for images on the Internet and in magazines or newspapers. See the table for more suggestions of the kinds of items to gather. Ask the children, their families and friends to help you build the classroom collection. A sample letter to families that includes information about sending in a variety of materials related to simple machines appears at the beginning of this *Teaching Guide*. Find out if children have any family members who have a career or hobby where they use simple machines. If so, invite them to visit the classroom to talk with the children about what they do.

Build on children's natural interest in simple machines as the simple machines collection arrives in the classroom. Think about how to store and display the collection so that the materials are available for children to explore. Observe children carefully as they explore the simple machines. Call attention to

questions they have or things they notice about them. Children need time to explore and talk about simple machines before beginning to engage in any formal investigations.

As children explore toys, materials, and pictures related to simple machines, observe and talk with them about what they are noticing and doing. Use open-ended questions and prompts to encourage discussion. Write children's responses on chart paper to encourage reading and writing.

What do you notice about the simple machines in the collection?

How can you use the simple machines?

What do the simple machines help you do?

How can the simple machines work together?

How do you think someone might use this simple machine at work?

What simple machines do you notice around your home or neighborhood?

Do you know anyone who uses simple machines?

Have you seen a simple machine like this before? Where did you see it?

> **What other open-ended questions or prompts can you use to stimulate questions about simple machines with the children in your class?**

<table>
<tr><td>

Objects and Materials
Lemon press
Small boards
Paper towel tubes
Water bottles
  with caps
Cardboard
Corkscrew
Gutter pieces
Garlic press
Chopsticks
Tweezers

</td><td>

Nuts and bolts
Scissors
Screws
Screwdriver
Screwdriver bits
Potato ricer
Jars with lids
Hole punchers
Tongs
Pliers
Nutcracker
Large triangle blocks

</td><td>

Large rectangle blocks
Small blocks
Hammer
Pictures and Videos
Interesting simple
  machines
Simple machines
  being used
Simple machines in
  your home
Simple machines in
  your community

</td></tr>
</table>

Children's questions will help you decide what experiences to offer and which investigations to pursue. During a group discussion, ask, "What should we try to find out about simple machines?" Record children's questions on a chart and add to the list of questions as the study progresses.

Model your own curiosity by wondering aloud, "I wonder what this pulley can help me lift."

Help younger children, or those with limited experiences, to verbalize their ideas and formulate questions. If a child says, "The ball goes down the ramp fast, but the block gets stuck," you could say, "Hmmm. It sounds like you are wondering about how different things move down a ramp. Let's add that question to our chart so we can find out."

Preparing for Wow! Experiences

The "At a Glance" pages list these suggested Wow! Experiences, which require some advanced planning.

Investigation 1:	Day 2: Take a walk to look for different kinds of inclined planes around the neighborhood.
	Day 5: Site visit to a local skate park to see how inclined planes are used
Investigation 2:	Day 3: Classroom visitor who is a chef or who cooks
Investigation 3:	Day 3: Site visit to a tire shop or another place where tires are changed
Investigation 4:	Day 2: Visit from a family member who will cook with the children using knives
	Day 3: Classroom visitor who roller skates
	Day 4: Take a walk to look for all kinds of simple machines.
Investigation 5:	Day 1: Classroom visitor who is a carpenter or woodworker
	Day 3: Site visit to a bike shop to see complex machines
	Day 4: Classroom visitor who is a mover or a delivery worker
Celebrating Learning:	Day 2: Family members and guests visit for the celebration.

Exploring the Topic

What do we know about simple machines?

Vocabulary—English: *force, simple machine, inclined plane, lever, screw, pulley, wedge, wheel and axle, operate, manual, investigate*

	Day 1	Day 2	Day 3
Interest Areas	**Discovery:** simple machines from the collection	**Library:** books that feature simple machines	**Art:** pictures of simple machines from around the classroom
Question of the Day	What does this feel like? (Share a feely box with a small simple machine.)	What is something heavy?	How do you use this simple machine? (Show tongs.)
Large Group	**Song:** "I've Got a Friend" **Discussion and Shared Writing:** What Do We Know About Simple Machines? **Materials:** *Mighty Minutes* 164, "I've Got a Friend"; "What We Know About Simple Machines" chart; simple machines	**Movement:** Let's Do a Hand Dance **Discussion and Shared Writing:** Introducing Simple Machines **Materials:** *Mighty Minutes* 112, "Let's Do a Hand Dance"; simple machines; book that shows various simple machines; chart paper	**Game:** Clap the Beat **Discussion and Shared Writing:** Simple Machines in the Classroom **Materials:** *Mighty Minutes* 59, "Clap the Beat"; simple machines; chart paper
Read-Aloud	*Don't Say a Word, Mamá* *Book Discussion Card* 57 (first read-aloud)	Reread the book from large group time.	Fiction book from the "Children's Books" list that talks about imagination
Small Group	**Option 1: Treasure Hunt** *Intentional Teaching Card* M87, "Treasure Hunt"; treasure items; paper; pencils **Option 2: Where's the Beanbag?** *Intentional Teaching Card* M56, "Where's the Beanbag?"; beanbags; basket or tub; masking tape; chart paper; marker	**Option 1: Sink or Float?** *Intentional Teaching Card* M81, "Sink or Float?"; plastic floor covering; large clear containers of water; two trays or plates; a variety of objects that might sink or float **Option 2: Let's Go Fishing** *Intentional Teaching Card* M39, "Let's Go Fishing"; child-sized fishing poles; set of fish cards; paper clips	**Option 1: Walk a Letter** *Intentional Teaching Card* LL17, "Walk a Letter"; masking tape; alphabet cards or an alphabet chart; chart paper; marker **Option 2: Stick Letters** *Intentional Teaching Card* LL28, "Stick Letters"; sticks; alphabet cards
Mighty Minutes®	*Mighty Minutes* 151, "Syllable Surprise"	*Mighty Minutes* 149, "Willy's Week"	*Mighty Minutes* 88, "Disappearing Rhymes"

What do we want to find out?

Spanish: *fuerza, máquinas simples, plano inclinado, palanca, tornillo, polea, cuña, rueda y eje, operar, manual, investigar*

Day 4	Day 5	Make Time for…
Discovery: handheld simple machines; camera	**Library:** fiction and nonfiction books that feature simple machines	## Outdoor Experiences • Bring simple machines from the collection outdoors for the children to explore. **Physical Fun** • Review *Intentional Teaching Card* P37, "Wonderful Warm-Ups." Follow the guidance on the card.
Is this a simple machine? (Show a machine that is not a simple machine.)	What do you want to find out about simple machines?	
Game: Syllable Stroll **Discussion and Shared Writing:** Machines and Simple Machines **Materials:** *Mighty Minutes* 155, "Syllable Stroll"; the "What We Know About Simple Machines" chart; simple machines	**Movement:** Hop the Circle **Discussion and Shared Writing:** What Do We Want to Find Out About Simple Machines? **Materials:** *Mighty Minutes* 144, "Hop the Circle"; "What We Know About Simple Machines" chart	## Family Partnerships • Introduce the study to families by sending a letter of explanation. Ask them to bring in items such as household simple machines (e.g., lemon squeezer, tongs, tweezers, and screw-top bottles) and books or photos of simple machines to add to the classroom collection. • Encourage families to help their children look around their homes for simple machines they use.
My Neighbors and Their Simple Machines	*A Farmer's Life for Me*	
Option 1: Action Patterns *Intentional Teaching Card* M35, "Action Patterns"; action cards; pocket chart **Option 2: Pots & Pans Band** *Intentional Teaching Card* M80, "Pots & Pans Band"; variety of pots, pans, and bowls; wooden spoons; plastic spatulas	**Option 1: Marble Mat** *Intentional Teaching Card* M82, "Marble Mat"; bath mat with suction cups aligned in rows; numeral cards 1–20; marbles; masking tape **Option 2: Fishing Trip** *Intentional Teaching Card* M63, "Fishing Trip"; fish cards; numeral cards; bucket; dry erase board and marker	## Wow! Experiences • Research local skate parks or other facilities that use inclined planes for the children to visit next week.
Mighty Minutes 188, "Swim, Bike, Run"	*Mighty Minutes* 17, "Leaping Sounds"	

What do we know about simple machines? What do we want to find out?

Vocabulary

English: *force; See Book Discussion Card 57, Don't Say a Word Mamá, for additional words.*

Spanish: *fuerza*

Question of the Day: What does this feel like? (Share a feely box with a small simple machine.)

Large Group

Opening Routine:

- Sing a welcome song and talk about who's here.

Song: "I've Got a Friend"

- Use *Mighty Minutes* 164, "I've Got a Friend." Follow the guidance on the card.

Discussion and Shared Writing: What Do We Know About Simple Machines?

- Review the question of the day and invite the children to describe the simple machine in the feely box.

- Show the children the simple machine from the feely box along with the collection of simple machines. Invite each child to choose one simple machine and pass it around for others to examine.

- As the children are examining the simple machines, ask questions and notice their observations.

- Ask questions such as:
  "Where have you seen something like this?"
  "What do you think this is used for?"
  "What size is this?"
  "How could this help someone?"
  "Why do you think this simple machine works like that?"

- Record the children's responses on a chart labeled "What We Know About Simple Machines." Save this chart for later use.

> **Remember to use correct terminology when talking about the components of simple machines. See *Intentional Teaching Card* LL43 "Introducing New Vocabulary" for additional support.**

Before transitioning to interest areas, talk about the collection of simple machines that is available in the Discovery area and how children can use the simple machines.

Choice Time

As you interact with children in the interest areas, make time to do the following:

- Observe how children explore the simple machines in the Discovery area.

- As the children make observations, support them to turn their observations into statements to add to the chart, e.g., "You noticed that the tongs and the scissors were both levers but they look different. We can add 'There are different kinds of levers.' to our chart."

- Talk with the children about the simple machines in the Discovery area.

- Introduce the word *force* into the conversation. Define *force* as "when you push, pull, or squeeze."

- Invite the children to experiment using different kinds of force with different classroom objects. For example, you can invite them to experiment with pushing a ball as you point out how the ball moves differently when you use a little force or a lot of force.

Read-Aloud

Read *Don't Say a Word, Mamá.*

- Use *Book Discussion Card* 57, *Don't Say a Word, Mamá.* Follow the guidance for the first read-aloud.

Small-Group

Option 1: Treasure Hunt

- Review *Intentional Teaching Card* M87, "Treasure Hunt." Follow the guidance on the card.

Option 2: Where's the Beanbag?

- Review *Intentional Teaching Card* M56, "Where's the Beanbag?" Follow the guidance on the card.

Mighty Minutes®

- Use *Mighty Minutes* 151, "Syllable Surprise." Follow the guidance on the card using items from the simple machine collection.

Large-Group Roundup

- Recall the day's events.

- Display the collection of simple machines from the Discovery area. Invite the children who explored the simple machines to share what they observed.

What do we know about simple machines? What do we want to find out?

Vocabulary

English: *simple machine, inclined plane, lever, screw, pulley, wedge, wheel and axle*

Spanish: *máquinas simples, plano inclinado, palanca, tornillo, polea, cuña, rueda y eje*

Question of the Day: What is something heavy?

Large Group

Opening Routine:

- Sing a welcome song and talk about who's here.

English-Language Learners
Observe English-language learners carefully when the class is singing together. Children who have not previously spoken English around others often begin using the language for the first time when singing with a group.

Movement: Let's Do a Hand Dance

- Use *Mighty Minutes* 112, "Let's Do a Hand Dance." Follow the guidance on the card.

Discussion and Shared Writing: Introducing Simple Machines

- Review the question of the day. Say, "I wonder what could help us move or lift all of those heavy things." Ask the children to suggest their ideas.

- Show the children examples of simple machines from the collection. Invite children to examine the objects closely.

- Explain that there are types of *simple machines* that can help you lift or move heavy things and make other types of work easier.

- Take a picture walk through a book that shows people using various types of simple machines. Point out each type of simple machine, introduce its name, and talk about what it is used for, e.g., "This is called an inclined plane. The delivery man is using it to help him carry that big load of vegetables up to the store."

- Remind the children of the heavy things that they named for the question of the day.

- Ask, "Which simple machine do you think could help us move those heavy things?" Record the children's responses on the "What We Know About Simple Machines Chart."

English-Language Learners
Show children an example of each type of simple machine as you name it.

Before transitioning to interest areas, tell the children that there are books about simple machines in the Library area for the children to continue exploring.

Choice Time

As you interact with children in the interest areas, make time to do the following:

- Observe the children who are exploring the books about simple machines in the Library area. Write down any questions or observations the children make about simple machines.

- As children are playing, point out any simple machines that you notice them using in the classroom areas. Tell them the name of the simple machine and talk about how they are using it.

- Ask open-ended questions that encourage the children to notice the different uses and characteristics of simple machines. For example, you might say, "This page shows all different kinds of inclined planes. What is the same about all of them?"

Read-Aloud

- Read the book that you introduced during large-group time. Invite the children to talk about how each type of simple machine is being used.

Small-Group

Option 1: Sink or Float?

- Review *Intentional Teaching Card* M81, "Sink or Float?" Follow the guidance on the card.

Option 2: Let's Go Fishing

- Review *Intentional Teaching Card* M39, "Let's Go Fishing." Follow the guidance on the card.

- Explain that a fishing pole is a lever, which is a type of simple machine.

Mighty Minutes®

- Use *Mighty Minutes* 149, "Willy's Week." Follow the guidance on the card.

Large-Group Roundup

- Recall the day's events
- Invite the children who explored books that featured simple machines in the Library area to share what they discovered.

What do we know about simple machines? What do we want to find out?

Vocabulary

English: *operate*

Spanish: *operar*

Question of the Day: How do you use this simple machine? (Show tongs.)

Large Group

Opening Routine:

- Sing a welcome song and talk about who's here.

Game: Clap the Beat

- Use *Mighty Minutes* 59, "Clap the Beat." Follow the guidance on the card.

Discussion and Shared Writing: Simple Machines in the Classroom

- Review the question of the day. Show the children simple machines from the collection and invite them to demonstrate how to use them.

- As you discuss how to use each simple machine, introduce the word *operate*. Explain that *operate* means "to make something work."

- Say, "I wonder if there are simple machines that we use in the classroom."

- Invite the children to walk around each interest area and look for simple machines. Take photos of the simple machines found around the room.

> **Identify and take photos of simple machines in the classroom. Print out the photos and add them to the Art area.**

- Ask, "What simple machines did you find?" Record the children's answers on a sheet of chart paper.

Before transitioning to interest areas, talk with the children about the photos of classroom simple machines that are displayed in the Art area and how they can use them as inspiration for their art.

Choice Time

As you interact with children in the interest areas, make time to do the following:

- Point out the photos of the simple machines that are displayed in the Art area. Talk with the children about how they can use them as inspiration for their art.

  Use *Intentional Teaching Card* LL45, "Observational Drawing," for guidance on supporting children's observational drawings.

- Encourage the children to notice the different parts and characteristics of each simple machine.

- Ask questions and make comments about their art and the simple machines that encourage the children to think about how they are using them as inspiration such as "I see that you made a big spiral on your paper; can you tell me about that?"

Read-Aloud

- Choose a book that talks about imagination from the "Children's Books" list found on pages 109–118. See the accompanying guidance for sharing the book with children.

English-Language Learners
Breaking a long reading into two or more segments helps English-language learners as well as English-speaking children stay focused and better able to comprehend the book.

Small-Group

Option 1: Walk a Letter

- Review *Intentional Teaching Card* LL17, "Walk a Letter." Follow the guidance on the card.

Option 2: Stick Letters

- Review *Intentional Teaching Card* LL28, "Stick Letters." Follow the guidance on the card.

Mighty Minutes®

- Use *Mighty Minutes* 88, "Disappearing Rhymes." Follow the guidance on the card.

English-Language Learners
Accept approximations of sounds as children try to identify English words that rhyme.

Large-Group Roundup

- Recall the day's events.
- Remind the children of the simple machines they found during large-group time. Talk about how they used them during the day.

- Invite the children who created art inspired by the photos of simple machines to share their work.

What do we know about simple machines?
What do we want to find out?

Vocabulary

English: *manual*

Spanish: *manual*

Question of the Day: Is this a simple machine?
(Show a machine that is not a simple machine.)

Large Group

Opening Routine:

- Sing a welcome song and talk about who's here.

Game: Syllable Stroll

- Use *Mighty Minutes* 155, "Syllable Stroll." Follow the guidance on the card.

Discussion and Shared Writing: Machines and Simple Machines

- Review the question of the day.

- Explain that not all *machines* are simple machines. Give a few examples of different kinds of machines that are a combination of tools, e.g., vehicles, computers, televisions, radios, etc.

- Display the machine from the question of the day and ask, "What is the difference between this machine and a simple machine?" Record the children's responses on the "What We Know About Simple Machines" chart.

- During the discussion, introduce the word *manual*. Explain that *manual* means that "you make it work with your body, and it does not use batteries or electricity." Explain that all simple machines are manual machines.

- Pass around a few simple machines and discuss how you operate them manually.

Before transitioning to interest areas, talk with the children about the selection of simple machines in the Discovery area.

Choice Time

As you interact with children in the interest areas, make time to do the following:

- Invite the children to explore how to use the simple machines.

- Take photos of the children using each of the simple machines.

- Discuss how the children are using their hands to operate the simple machines. For example, "I see that you are using your fingers to turn the bolt onto the nut."

- Ask open-ended questions to encourage the children to think about how they are using the simple machines.

Read-Aloud

Read *My Neighbors and Their Simple Machines*.

• Invite the children to point out and name the simple machines they see.

Small-Group

Option 1: Action Patterns

• Review *Intentional Teaching Card* M35, "Action Patterns." Follow the guidance on the card.

Option 2: Pots and Pans Band

• Review *Intentional Teaching Card* M80, "Pots and Pans Band." Follow the guidance on the card.

Mighty Minutes®

• Use *Mighty Minutes* 188, "Swim, Bike, Run." Follow the guidance on the card.

• Talk with the children about how bicycles are *manual* because they are operated using power from your body.

Large-Group Roundup

• Recall the day's events.

• Share the photos of the children using different simple machines in the Discovery area. Invite the children to explain how they used their hands to push, pull, squeeze, and turn the simple machines.

What do we know about simple machines? What do we want to find out?

Vocabulary

English: *investigate*

Spanish: *investigar*

Question of the Day: What do you want to find out about simple machines?

Large Group

Opening Routine:

- Sing a welcome song and talk about who's here.

Movement: Hop the Circle

- Use *Mighty Minutes* 144, "Hop the Circle." Follow the guidance on the card.

Discussion and Shared Writing: What Do We Want to Find Out About Simple Machines?

- Review the "What We Know About Simple Machines" chart.

- Say, "We already know so many things about simple machines. Let's think about what we would like to find out about them."

- Invite the children to ask questions and share their ideas.

- Record their responses on a chart titled "What Do We Want to Find Out About Simple Machines?" Support the children to turn their observations into questions. For example, if a child says, "Some screws have an x on top and some just have a line," you can respond, "You noticed that there are different types of screws. I'll write 'How are screws different?' on the chart."

- Review the question of the day and add any additional questions to the chart.

- Explain that the children will *investigate* each type of simple machine to "learn more about them" and answer their questions on the chart.

Before transitioning to interest areas, remind the children to explore the books about simple machines in the Library area.

Choice Time

As you interact with children in the interest areas, make time to do the following:

- Observe what the children are noticing or paying attention to in the books about simple machines.

- Post the "What Do We Want to Find Out About Simple Machines?" chart near the Library area.

- As the children are exploring books about simple machines, invite them to add questions to the chart.

English-Language Learners
As English-language learners attempt to produce sounds in English, keep in mind that some sounds may be new or difficult for them to produce. You might find that you need to demonstrate and explain lip and tongue placement to help children learn how to create these new sounds.

Read-Aloud

- Read *A Farmer's Life for Me* from the "Children's Books" list on pages 109–118. See the accompanying guidance for ideas on sharing the book with children.

English-Language Learners
When possible, read a book in a child's home language before reading it aloud in English.

Small-Group

Option 1: Marble Mat

- Review *Intentional Teaching Card* M82, "Marble Mat." Follow the guidance on the card.

Option 2: Fishing Trip

- Review *Intentional Teaching Card* M63, "Fishing Trip." Follow the guidance on the card.

Mighty Minutes®

- Use *Mighty Minutes* 17, "Leaping Sounds." Follow the guidance on the card.

Large-Group Roundup

- Recall the day's events.

- Review the "What Do We Want to Find Out About Simple Machines?" chart.

- Remind the children that they will be investigating these questions to learn more about simple machines.

Investigating the Topic

Introduction

You have already started lists of children's ideas and questions about simple machines. As you implement the study, you will design investigations that help the children expand their ideas, find answers to their questions, and learn important skills and concepts. This section has daily plans for investigating questions that children ask. Do not be limited by these suggestions. Use them as inspiration to design experiences tailored to your own group of children and the resources in your school and community. While it is important to respond to children's ideas and follow their lead as their thinking evolves, it is also important for you to organize the study and plan for possibilities. Be sure to review the "At a Glance" pages for suggested Wow! Experiences, as these events require some advance planning.

Investigation 1

How do inclined planes help us move things?

Vocabulary—English: *load, tilt, angle, friction, surface*

	Day 1	**Day 2**	**Day 3**
Interest Areas	**Blocks:** photos of ramps and inclined planes in the community	**Blocks:** large, sturdy inclined plane	**Blocks:** materials to make inclined planes
Question of the Day	How can you move this box? (Show a heavy box.)	What can we use to make an inclined plane?	What is something that rolls?
Large Group	**Game:** Heavy & Light **Discussion and Shared Writing:** Exploring Inclined Planes **Materials:** *Mighty Minutes* 179, "Heavy & Light"; flat boards; blocks; "What Do We Want to Find Out About Simple Machines?" chart	**Song:** "Abby Had an Anteater" **Discussion and Shared Writing:** Inclined Planes in the Neighborhood **Materials:** *Mighty Minutes* 103, "Abby Had an Anteater"; clipboards; paper; pencils; camera; chart paper	**Movement:** Action Counting **Discussion and Shared Writing:** Long and Short Inclined Planes **Materials:** *Mighty Minutes* 140, "Action Counting"; flat planes; blocks; classroom items that roll or slide; chart paper
Read-Aloud	*Don't Say a Word, Mamá* *Book Discussion Card* 57 (second read-aloud)	*Highlights High Five Bilingüe™, ¡Para ti!/For You!* *Book Conversation Card* 02	Book about families from the "Children's Books" list
Small Group	**Option 1: I'm Thinking of a Shape** *Intentional Teaching Card* M20, "I'm Thinking of a Shape"; geometric solids; empty containers of different sizes **Option 2: Buried Shapes** *Intentional Teaching Card* M30, "Buried Shapes"; card stock or heavy paper; attribute blocks; three containers; glue; sandbox or tub of sand; small brushes	**Option 1: How Many in the Scoop?** *Intentional Teaching Card* M92, "How Many in the Scoop?"; small scoop; jar or box; small classroom items **Option 2: More or Fewer Towers** *Intentional Teaching Card* M59, "More or Fewer Towers"; interlocking cubes; More/Fewer spinner; numeral/quantity cards; die	**Option 1: Silly Names** *Intentional Teaching Card* LL19, "Silly Names"; chart paper; sentence strips or sticky notes **Option 2: Tongue Twisters** *Intentional Teaching Card* LL16, "Tongue Twisters"; chart paper, markers
Mighty Minutes®	*Mighty Minutes* 14, "Scat Singing"	*Mighty Minutes* 183, "Just Move One"	*Mighty Minutes* 111, "I Love Me"

Day 4	Day 5	Make Time for...
Sand and Water: materials to make inclined planes	**Blocks:** pictures of inclined planes at a skate park	## Outdoor Experiences
Where did you see an inclined plane today?	Which of these is an inclined plane you play on? (Show pictures of different inclined planes including a slide and a ramp at a skate park.)	• Provide materials to make inclined planes outdoors. **Physical Fun** • Review *Intentional Teaching Card* P38, "Body Bump." Follow the guidance on the card.
Song: "Clap a Friend's Name" **Discussion and Shared Writing:** Surface of Inclined Planes **Materials:** *Mighty Minutes* 40, "Clap a Friend's Name"; pictures of a water slide and loading ramp; chart paper; blocks	**Game:** Listen For Your Name **Discussion and Shared Writing:** Site Visit to the Skate Park **Materials:** *Mighty Minutes* 85, "Listen For Your Name"; picture of a skate park; chart from yesterday's large-group roundup; clipboards; paper; pencils; camera	## Family Partnerships • Invite families to contribute large cardboard boxes to use to create inclined planes. • Invite families to accompany the class on the site visit to the skate park (Day 5).
Don't Say a Word, Mamá *Book Discussion Card* 57 (third read-aloud)	Reread book from Day 3.	## Wow! Experiences • Day 2: Take a walk to look for inclined planes • Day 5: Site visit to a local skate park
Option 1: Can You Find It? *Intentional Teaching Card* M51, "Can You Find It?"; small objects typically found in a classroom **Option 2: We're Going on an Adventure** *Intentional Teaching Card* M36, "We're Going on an Adventure"; materials to make an adventure course; photographs with geographic features	**Option 1: Patterns Under Cover** *Intentional Teaching Card* M38, "Patterns Under Cover"; counters in a variety of colors; paper cup; cardboard divider **Option 2: Perler Patterns** *Intentional Teaching Card* M85, "Perler Patterns"; large perler beads; square or rectangle pegboards; parchment or iron paper; iron	**When preparing for site visits, special visitors, or other changes to the typical classroom routine, review *Intentional Teaching Card* SE32, "Planning for Change," to help prepare children for the upcoming change.**
Mighty Minutes 105, "Popping Popcorn"	*Mighty Minutes* 195, "Don't Forget Your Ears"	**Preparing for the Week:** Use a smooth piece of wood or another flat surface to create a sturdy inclined plane that will not bend as children push things up it. Add texture to increase the friction on some of your planes by adding sand, fabric, or carpet samples.

How do inclined planes help us move things?

Vocabulary

English: *load*; See Book Discussion Card 57, *Don't Say a Word Mamá*, for additional words.

Spanish: carga

Question of the Day: How can you move this box? (Show a heavy box.)

Large Group

Opening Routine:

- Sing a welcome song and talk about who's here.

Game: Heavy Box

- Use *Mighty Minutes* 179, "Heavy & Light." Follow the guidance on the card.

- Introduce the word *load* as children are pretending to put different things in the box. Explain that *load* means "something that is being carried."

English-Language Learners
Whenever possible, make an intentional effort to explain, define, or show children the meaning of new and key vocabulary words throughout the day. This technique helps reinforce understanding for all children.

Discussion and Shared Writing: Exploring Inclined Planes

- Prior to the beginning of large-group time, use flat boards and blocks to set up a few inclined planes in the large-group area.

- Refer to the chart "What Do We Want to Find Out About Simple Machines?" and review the questions related to inclined planes.

- Explain that an *inclined plane* is "a flat object that is higher on one end."

- Show the children a few examples of people using inclined planes such as an adult pushing a stroller up a ramp or children going down a slide.

- Point out the inclined planes that you set up. Ask, "What could we move up and down on our inclined planes?" Record the children's answers.

- Invite the children to choose items from the classroom to move up or down the inclined planes.

- As they experiment, discuss how the items move on the inclined planes and invite the children to add more ideas to the chart.

Before transitioning to interest areas, talk about the photos of different inclined planes in the Block area and how the children can use them for inspiration as they build.

Choice Time

As you interact with children in the interest areas, make time to do the following:

- Observe how the children incorporate inclined planes into the structures they are building.

- Point out any inclined planes that you notice and talk about how they were made. For example, you may say, "I see you put the flat block on top of the rectangle block to make an inclined plane leading into your structure. What will you use that for?"

Read-Aloud

Read *Don't Say a Word, Mamá.*

- Use *Book Discussion Card 57, Don't Say a Word, Mamá.* Follow the guidance for the second read-aloud.

Small-Group

Option 1: I'm Thinking of a Shape

- Review *Intentional Teaching Card* M20, "I'm Thinking of a Shape." Follow the guidance on the card.

Option 2: Buried Shapes

- Review *Intentional Teaching Card* M30, "Buried Shapes." Follow the guidance on the card.

Mighty Minutes®

- Use *Mighty Minutes* 14, "Scat Singing." Follow the guidance on the card.

Large-Group Roundup

- Recall the day's events.
- Invite the children who incorporated inclined planes into their block building to share their experiences.

- Choose several blocks from the classroom set and invite children to demonstrate how they can use them to create different kinds of inclined planes.

How do inclined planes help us move things?

Vocabulary

English: *tilt*

Spanish: *declive*

Question of the Day: What can we use to make an inclined plane?

Large Group

Opening Routine:

- Sing a welcome song and talk about who's here.

Song: "Abby Had an Anteater"

- Use *Mighty Minutes* 103, "Abby Had an Anteater." Follow the guidance on the card.

Discussion and Shared Writing: Inclined Planes in the Neighborhood

- Explain, "We will be taking a walk around the neighborhood today to look for inclined planes."

- Point out something that you are interested in seeing, e.g., "I am going to look at the front of buildings to see which ones have ramps."

- Invite the children to share what they are interested in seeing as well.

- During the walk, take photos of the inclined planes the children find.

> **Use *Intentional Teaching Card* LL45, "Observational Drawing." Follow the guidance on the card and invite the children to draw the inclined planes they find.**

- After the walk, ask, "What inclined planes did you see in our neighborhood?" Record the children's answers.

Before transitioning to interest areas, point out the inclined plane in the Block area and talk about how the children can use it.

Choice Time

As you interact with children in the interest areas, make time to do the following:

- Invite the children to push different items up the ramp in the Block area.

- Ask the children to compare lifting heavy items and pushing them up the ramp. For example you may say, "We need to move this heavy box of blocks to the top of this shelf. Can you lift it all the way up to there? Now try pushing it up the ramp. Which way was easier?"

- Raise and lower the ramp and talk with the children about how this makes it easier or harder to push things up. During the conversation, introduce the word *tilt*. Explain that *tilt* means "to raise or lower something so that it is higher on one end."

Read-Aloud

Read *Highlights High Five Bilingüe*™, *¡Para ti!/For You!*

- Choose a few literacy experiences to share with children.

- Use *Book Conversation Card* 02, *¡Para ti!/For You!* Follow the guidance on the card.

Small-Group

Option 1: How Many in the Scoop?

- Review *Intentional Teaching Card* M92, "How Many in the Scoop?" Follow the guidance on the card.

Option 2: More or Fewer Towers

- Review *Intentional Teaching Card* M59, "More or Fewer Towers." Follow the guidance on the card.

Mighty Minutes®

- Use *Mighty Minutes* 183, "Just Move One." Follow the guidance on the card.

Activities that encourage children to use impulse control give children an opportunity to practice self-regulation which is an important executive function skill.

Large-Group Roundup

- Recall the day's events.

- Review the question of the day. Share the photos of inclined planes from your neighborhood walk and discuss how they are made.

- Invite children who experimented with the inclined plane in the Block area to share their observations.

How do inclined planes help us move things?

Vocabulary

English: *angle*

Spanish: *ángulo*

Question of the Day: What is something that rolls?

Large Group

Opening Routine:

- Sing a welcome song and talk about who's here.

Movement: Action Counting

- Use *Mighty Minutes* 140, "Action Counting." Follow the guidance on the card.

Discussion and Shared Writing: Long and Short Inclined Planes

- Show the children two flat planes that you can use to make inclined planes, one short and one long.

- Invite the children to use blocks to measure the planes and compare their lengths.

- Use the planes to make two inclined planes that are the same height.

- Ask, "What is the difference between these two inclined planes?" Record children's answers on a sheet of chart paper.

- As you discuss the inclined planes, introduce the word *angle*. Explain that an *angle* is "made where a plane touches another plane."

- Show the children one item such as a block, car, or ball. Roll or slide it down each of the inclined planes and ask, "How did it move differently on the long and short inclined planes?" Record the children's answers.

English-Language Learners
English-language learners must gain language proficiency in both social and academic English to be successful in school. Social language enables children to interact effectively with others and form friendships. Academic language enables children to understand concepts and explain their thinking.

Before transitioning to interest areas, talk with the children about the materials to make inclined planes that are available in the Block area. Discuss how to use them to make long and short inclined planes.

Choice Time

As you interact with children in the interest areas, make time to do the following:

- Support the children to create inclined planes of different sizes using the materials in the Block area.

- Observe how the children are rolling or sliding materials up and down the inclined planes they create.

- Ask open-ended questions to encourage children to notice and compare how materials move down their inclined planes.

See *Intentional Teaching Card* **M84, "Ramp Experiments," for guidance on how to support children in comparing how materials move down the inclined planes.**

- Review the question of the day and invite children to roll the items they named up or down an inclined plane.

Read-Aloud

- Choose a book about families from the "Children's Books" list on pages 109–118. See the accompanying guidance for ideas on sharing the book with children.

Small-Group

Option 1: Silly Names

- Review *Intentional Teaching Card* LL19, "Silly Names." Follow the guidance on the card.

Option 2: Tongue Twisters

- Review *Intentional Teaching Card* LL16, "Tongue Twisters." Follow the guidance on the card.

Mighty Minutes®

- Use *Mighty Minutes* 111, "I Love Me." Follow the guidance on the card.

Large-Group Roundup

- Recall the day's events.

- Invite children who experimented with inclined planes in the Block area to share their observations.

How do inclined planes help us move things?

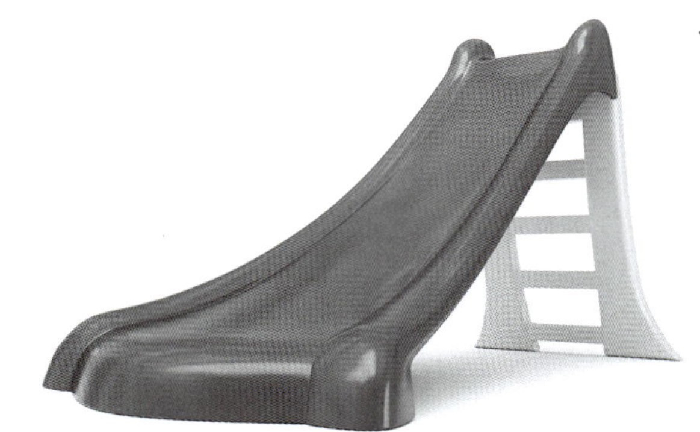

Vocabulary

English: *friction;* See *Book Discussion Card 57, Don't Say a Word Mamá,* for additional words.

Spanish: *fricción*

Question of the Day: Where did you see an inclined plane today?

Large Group

Opening Routine:

- Sing a welcome song and talk about who's here.

Song: "Clap a Friend's Name"

- Use *Mighty Minutes* 40, "Clap a Friend's Name." Follow the guidance on the card.

Discussion and Shared Writing: Surface of Inclined Planes

- Show the children a picture of a water slide and a loading ramp.

- Point out that the surface of the loading ramp is rough and gritty and that the water slide is smooth and wet.

- Ask, "Why is it useful to make a loading ramp rough and gritty? What would happen if the water slide wasn't smooth and wet?" Document the children's responses on a sheet of chart paper.

- Introduce the word *friction.* Explain that *friction* is "the force that slows things down when they rub together."

> **Refer to the *Teaching Guide featuring the Boxes Study* for more ideas about exploring *friction* with children.**

- Give each child a block and invite the children to slide their blocks on the carpet. Ask, "Do you think the block would slide further on the carpet or on the table?" Then ask the children to slide the blocks on a smooth surface such as a table or the tile floor.

- Ask, "Did your block slide further on the table or the carpet?" Record the children's responses and talk about how the *friction* of the carpet slows the block down more than the *friction* of the table or floor.

Before transitioning to interest areas, talk about the smooth and rough inclined planes that are available in the Sand and Water area and how the children can use them.

Choice Time

As you interact with children in the interest areas, make time to do the following:

- Support the children to set up inclined planes in the Sand and Water area.

- Invite them to use the planes with sand, fabric, or carpet added to create inclined planes. Explain that these planes will increase the friction.

- Encourage the children to make predictions and compare how things move differently on the inclined planes with water and the ones with sand, fabric, or carpet.

- Invite children to try their own ideas of how to increase or reduce friction on the inclined planes.

Read-Aloud

Read *Don't Say a Word, Mamá.*

- Use *Book Discussion Card 57. Don't Say a Word, Mamá.* Follow the guidance for the third read-aloud.

Small-Group

Option 1: Can You Find It?

- Review *Intentional Teaching Card* M51, "Can You Find It?" Follow the guidance on the card.

Option 2: We're Going on an Adventure

- Review *Intentional Teaching Card* M36, "We're Going on an Adventure." Follow the guidance on the card.

Mighty Minutes®

- Use *Mighty Minutes* 105, "Popping Popcorn." Follow the guidance on the card.

Large-Group Roundup

- Recall the day's events.

- Review the question of the day and invite children to share where they saw an inclined plane.

- Invite the children who experimented with friction on inclined planes in the Sand and Water area to share their observations.

- Remind the children about tomorrow's site visit to the skate park. Ask, "What do you think we will see at the skate park?" and record the children's answers.

How do inclined planes help us move things?

Vocabulary

English: *surface*

Spanish: *superficie*

Question of the Day: Which of these is an inclined plane you play on? (Show pictures of different inclined planes including a slide and a ramp at a skate park.)

Large Group

Opening Routine:

- Sing a welcome song and talk about who's here.

Game: Listen For Your Name

- Use *Mighty Minutes* 85, "Listen For Your Name." Follow the guidance on the card.

Discussion and Shared Writing: Site Visit to the Skate Park

- Talk about the question of the day. Point to the picture of a skate park and explain that you will be visiting a skate park today to see how inclined planes are used there.

- Review the question from yesterday's large-group roundup and invite the children to add more ideas to the chart.

- Before the site visit, remind the children about expectations for their behavior.

See *Intentional Teaching Card* SE01, "Site Visits," for more information about preparing children for site visits.

- Give the children clipboard, paper, and pencils to document their observations during the site visit.

- Visit a local skate park to watch how skate boarders, roller skaters, or roller-bladers use the inclined planes.

- Encourage the children to use their paper and pencils to record what they see.

- In a safe area of the skate park, invite the children to touch the inclined planes.

- Introduce the word *surface*. Explain that *surface* means "the outside of something."

- Ask, "What does the surface of the inclined plane feel like?" Record the children's responses.

- Take photos or videos during the site visit for the children to view later.

Before transitioning to interest areas, talk about the pictures of the skate park that are displayed in the Block area and how children can use them for inspiration as they build.

Choice Time

As you interact with children in the interest areas, make time to do the following:

- Talk with the children about the different inclined planes they see in the photos of the skate park in the Block area.

- Notice how the children are using them for inspiration as they build.

- Ask open-ended questions that prompt children to think of new ways to use the blocks to represent inclined planes. Take photos of their work.

Read-Aloud

- Reread the story that you read on Day 3 of this investigation. Invite the children to share what they remember from the story.

> **Refer to *Intentional Teaching Card* LL06, "Dramatic Story Retelling," for ways to support children as they retell the story.**

Small-Group

Option 1: Patterns Under Cover

- Review *Intentional Teaching Card* M38, "Patterns Under Cover." Follow the guidance on the card.

Option 2: Perler Patterns

- Review *Intentional Teaching Card* M85, "Perler Patterns." Follow the guidance on the card.

Mighty Minutes®

- Use *Mighty Minutes* 195, "Don't Forget Your Ears." Follow the guidance on the card.

Large-Group Roundup

- Recall the day's events.

- Ask, "How did people play on the inclined planes at the skate park?" Record the children's responses.

- Invite the children who built inclined planes in the Block area to share their work.

Investigation 2

How are levers used?

Vocabulary—English: *fulcrum, tongs, chef, balance, tools*

	Day 1	Day 2	Day 3
Interest Areas	**Discovery:** materials to make levers	**Toys and Games:** variety of items that are large and small, e.g., feathers, pom poms, balls, etc.; large and small tweezers and tongs	**Cooking:** lemons, lemon squeezer, sugar, cups, pitcher, mixing spoon
Question of the Day	What is this? (Show a picture of a seesaw.)	Which of these is a lever? (Show tongs and another item that is not a lever.)	What is this used for? (Show a lemon squeezer.)
Large Group	**Game:** People Patterns **Discussion and Shared Writing:** Exploring Levers **Materials:** *Mighty Minutes* 65, "People Patterns"; picture of seesaw; blocks	**Game:** My Name, Too! **Discussion and Shared Writing:** Putting Two Levers Together **Materials:** *Mighty Minutes* 35, "My Name, Too!"; tongs; chart paper; classroom materials	**Movement:** The Name Dance **Discussion and Shared Writing:** Visitor Who is a Chef **Materials:** *Mighty Minutes* 60, "The Name Dance"; chart from yesterday's large-group roundup; cooking levers
Read-Aloud	Counting book from the "Children's Books" list	*Owen* Book Discussion Card 56 (first read-aloud)	Selection of a nonfiction book from the "Children's Books" list
Small Group	**Option 1: Photo Writing** *Intentional Teaching Card* LL57, "Photo Writing"; small clipboards with paper; pens or markers; variety of photos of levers **Option 2: Author & Illustrator** *Intentional Teaching Card* LL69, "Author & Illustrator"; example of a storybook in which the author and illustrator are different; cardboard or card stock; blank paper; pencils, crayons, or markers; bookbinding supplies	**Option 1: Mixing Paints** *Intentional Teaching Card* P30, "Mixing Paints"; white construction paper; paint; paintbrushes; tray; palette or large plate for mixing paint; familiar book with colorful illustrations **Option 2: Cutting With Scissors** *Intentional Teaching Card* P08, "Cutting With Scissors"; safety scissors; paper; thick, dark marker	**Option 1: Number Cards** *Intentional Teaching Card* M04, "Number Cards"; set of cards with a numeral and its number word printed on one side; buttons or other small manipulatives **Option 2: Ping-Pong Pick-Up** *Intentional Teaching Card* M79, "Ping-Pong Pick-Up"; table tennis balls; tongs; water for the water table
Mighty Minutes®	*Mighty Minutes* 157, "Up & Down on the Seesaw"	*Mighty Minutes* 172, "Bridge & Tunnel"	*Mighty Minutes* 168, "The Sounds We Found"

Day 4	Day 5	Make Time for…
Discovery: collection of levers to balance	**Art:** scissors; hole punchers; and staplers	## Outdoor Experiences • Bring large blocks or boards outside for the children to use to create and balance levers. **Physical Fun** • Review *Intentional Teaching Card* P20, "Body Shapes & Sizes." Follow the guidance on the card.
Which of these is heavier? (Show two items on a balance scale.)	Can you tear the paper on this line? (Provide a piece of paper with a straight line down the middle.)	
Game: Time's Up! **Discussion and Shared Writing:** Balance with a Moving Fulcrum **Materials:** *Mighty Minutes* 134, "Time's Up!"; balance scale; blocks; flat plane; chart paper	**Game:** 1, 2, 3, What Do I See? **Discussion and Shared Writing:** Paper and Levers **Materials:** *Mighty Minutes* 50, "1, 2, 3, What Do I See?"; chart paper; scissors; paper	## Family Partnerships • Invite a chef or family member who cooks to visit the classroom. • Encourage families to cook with their children at home.
Selection of an alphabet book from the "Children's Books" list	*Owen* *Book Discussion Card* 56 (second read-aloud)	## Wow! Experiences • Day 3: Visit from a chef or family member who cooks • Research tire shops or other places where people change tires for the children to visit next week.
Option 1: Asking Questions *Intentional Teaching Card* LL54, "Asking Questions"; chart paper; markers **Option 2: That's How You Do It!** *Intentional Teaching Card* LL78, "That's How You Do It!"; chart paper; markers; camera	**Option 1: Patterns** *Intentional Teaching Card* M14, "Patterns"; group of objects to be arranged in a pattern; examples of patterns; a pattern of flowers or bricks; construction paper; crayons or markers **Option 2: Picture Patterns** *Intentional Teaching Card* M45, "Picture Patterns"; a book or collection of photos of objects and animals that have patterns; digital camera; collage materials	
Mighty Minutes 153, "Washing Machine"	*Mighty Minutes* 31, "What's Inside the Box?"	

How are levers used?

Vocabulary

English: *fulcrum*
Spanish: *fulcro*
Question of the Day: What is this? (Show a picture of a seesaw.)

Large Group

Opening Routine:

- Sing a welcome song and talk about who's here.

Game: People Patterns

- Use *Mighty Minutes* 65, "People Patterns." Follow the guidance on the card.

Discussion and Shared Writing: Exploring Levers

- Review the question of the day. Explain that a seesaw is a type of lever.

- Introduce the word *fulcrum*. Explain that the *fulcrum* is the "point where the lever turns."

- Point to the *fulcrum* in the picture of the seesaw. Ask, "Where is the *fulcrum* on this lever?" Record the children's answers.

- Provide a variety of blocks, including long flat blocks and ask, "Can we use these blocks to make a lever like the seesaw?"

- Invite the children to arrange the blocks into a seesaw.

- Explain that this is just one type of lever and that you can make different types of levers by moving the fulcrum or putting two levers together.

Before transitioning to interest areas, show the children the lever and fulcrum materials that are available in the Discovery area and talk about how they can use them to make levers.

Choice Time

As you interact with children in the interest areas, make time to do the following:

- Support the children as they use the materials in the Discovery area to make levers.

- Encourage the children to move the fulcrum to different points of the lever. Ask, "How does the lever change when you move the fulcrum?" Record the children's responses.

- Take photos to document the levers the children create.

Read-Aloud

- Choose a counting book from the "Children's Books" list on pages 109–118. See the accompanying guidance for ideas on sharing the book with children.

English-Language Learners
Explain slang, idioms, and figures of speech that appear in children's books. Most young children are literal thinkers, so they may miss meaning or nuance in a story if they haven't heard common English expressions before or don't understand them.

Small-Group

Option 1: Photo Writing

- Review *Intentional Teaching Card* LL57, "Photo Writing." Follow the guidance on the card using photos of people who are using levers.

- Point out the levers in the photos and talk with the children about how they are being used.

Option 2: Author & Illustrator

- Review *Intentional Teaching Card* LL69, "Author & Illustrator." Follow the guidance on the card.

Mighty Minutes®

- Use *Mighty Minutes* 157, "Up & Down on the Seesaw." Follow the guidance on the card.

- Remind the children that a seesaw is a type of lever.

Large-Group Roundup

- Recall the day's events.
- Invite the children who made levers in the Discovery area to share their work.

How are levers used?

Vocabulary

English: *tongs;* See *Book Discussion Card 56, Owen,* for additional words.

Spanish: *pinzas*

Question of the Day: Which of these is a lever? (Show tongs and another item that is not a lever.)

Large Group

Opening Routine:

- Sing a welcome song and talk about who's here.

Game: My Name, Too!

- Use *Mighty Minutes* 35, "My Name, Too!" Follow the guidance on the card.

Discussion and Shared Writing: Putting Two Levers Together

- Review the question of the day. Show the children the *tongs* and explain that *tongs* are "a tool you squeeze to pick things up."

- Give each child an opportunity to touch and inspect the tongs. Explain that tongs are two levers put together with the fulcrum at one end.

- Ask, "What do you think we could pick up with this tool?" Record the children's answers on a sheet of chart paper.

- Show the children a basket that has a variety of classroom objects of varying sizes and weights.

- Invite the children to take turns using the tongs to pick up an item from the basket. Ask, "Was it easy or challenging to pick that up with tongs?"

- Create two groups of items, ones that were easy to pick up and ones that were challenging. Ask, "What do you notice about the items that were easy to pick up with the tongs? What about the challenging items?" Record the children's comments about the two groups.

Before transitioning to interest areas, talk about the levers and materials available in the Toys and Games area for children to experiment with and how they can use them.

Choice Time

As you interact with children in the interest areas, make time to do the following:

- Encourage the children to experiment picking up items with the different-sized levers.
- Ask the children to describe what type of item each lever is best at picking up.
- Encourage the children to share how they have seen the tweezers or tongs used in their homes.

English-Language Learners
Expanding a process is a higher-level skill that is often one of the most difficult for children to acquire. Children might be able to analyze a simple task before being able to express their thoughts in English. To help them, explain each of the steps in the process as it is completed. Have frequent, informal conversations with children about what they are doing.

Read-Aloud

Read *Owen.*

- Use *Book Discussion Card* 56, *Owen.* Follow the guidance for the first read-aloud.

Small-Group

Option 1: Mixing Paints

- Review *Intentional Teaching Card* P30, "Mixing Paints." Follow the guidance on the card.

Option 2: Cutting With Scissors

- Review *Intentional Teaching Card* P08, "Cutting With Scissors." Follow the guidance on the card.

Mighty Minutes®

- Use *Mighty Minutes* 172, "Bridge & Tunnel." Follow the guidance on the card.

Large-Group Roundup

- Recall the day's events.
- Invite the children who experimented with the levers in the Toys and Games area to share their observations.

- Explain that a visitor who works with tongs and other levers in the kitchen will be coming to the classroom tomorrow. Ask, "What questions would you like to ask our visitor?" Record the children's questions so you can review them together before the visit.

How are levers used?

Vocabulary

English: *chef*

Spanish: *chef*

Question of the Day: What is this used for? (Show a lemon squeezer.)

Large Group

Opening Routine:

- Sing a welcome song and talk about who's here.

Movement: The Name Dance

- Use *Mighty Minutes* 60, "The Name Dance." Follow the guidance on the back of the card where you keep a steady beat on a drum as the children dance their names.

Discussion and Shared Writing: Visitor Who is a Chef

- Introduce the visitor.

- Explain that the visitor is a *chef*, which means that she is "a person who cooks."

- Invite the visitor to explain her job and share what types of levers she uses.

- Display and review the children's questions from yesterday's large-group roundup. Record the visitor's responses on the chart.

- Invite the visitor to demonstrate how to use a few levers that are cooking tools and discuss how they help her.

English-Language Learners

If the visitor speaks any of the children's home languages, ask her to respond to questions in English and in any other languages in which she is proficient. Supporting children's home-language development helps them keep their cultural identities, stay attached to family traditions, and become bilingual.

Before transitioning to interest areas, talk with the children about the levers and ingredients that are available in the Cooking area for the children to use during choice time.

Choice Time

As you interact with children in the interest areas, make time to do the following:

> **See *Intentional Teaching Card* LL24, "Lemonade," for guidance on using the lemon squeezer to make lemonade with the children.**

- Review the question of the day.

- Ask the chef to demonstrate how to use the lemon squeezer to juice a lemon for the lemonade.

- Invite the children to take turns juicing the lemons with the lemon squeezer.

- Point out the parts of the lemon squeezer. Say, "The lemon squeezer has a fulcrum at one end. What other levers have we used that have a fulcrum at one end?"

Read-Aloud

- Choose a nonfiction book from the "Children's Books" list found on pages 109–118. See the accompanying guidance for sharing the book with children.

Small-Group

Option 1: Number Cards

- Review *Intentional Teaching Card* M04, "Number Cards." Follow the guidance on the card.

Option 2: Ping-Pong Pick-Up

- Review *Intentional Teaching Card* M79, "Ping-Pong Pick-Up." Follow the guidance on the card.

- Offer the children a variety of tongs or other levers as tools to pick up the table tennis balls.

Mighty Minutes®

- Use *Mighty Minutes* 168, "The Sounds We Found." Follow the guidance on the card.

Large-Group Roundup

- Recall the day's events.

- Invite the children who made lemonade to talk about the process.

- Have the children help you create a thank-you card for the visitor. Invite children to sign their names and add drawings to the card.

How are levers used?

Vocabulary

English: *balance*

Spanish: *equilibrio*

Question of the Day: Which of these is heavier? (Show two items on a balance scale.)

Large Group

Opening Routine:

- Sing a welcome song and talk about who's here.

Game: Alarm Clock

- Use *Mighty Minutes* 134, "Time's Up!" Follow the guidance on the card.

Discussion and Shared Writing: Balance with a Moving Fulcrum

- Review the question of the day. Discuss how the heavier item is lower on the scale and the lighter item is higher. Invite children to add more items to the scale to *balance* it. Explain that *balance* means "both sides are the same."

- Place a fulcrum in the middle of a long, flat plane such as sturdy piece of cardboard or a block.

- Place a few items on one side of the lever and ask, "How can we balance our lever?" Record the children's responses and invite them to try their ideas to balance the lever.

- Once the lever is balanced, ask, "What do you think will happen if we move the fulcrum to one side?" Continue to record the children's responses.

- Move the fulcrum to a new position and invite the children to add or remove items from each side until it is balanced.

Before transitioning to interest areas, talk with the children about the levers and balancing materials that are available in the Discovery area.

Choice Time

As you interact with children in the interest areas, make time to do the following:

- Observe how the children are creating and balancing levers in the Discovery area.

- Encourage the children to move the fulcrum of their levers and notice what happens to the lever's balance.

- Make comments and ask open-ended questions about what you observe the children doing. For example, you might say, "I see that you are moving the fulcrum all the way to one side of your lever. Hmm, I wonder what you will need to use to balance your lever now. What are you going to place on the shorter side of the lever?"

English-Language Learners
Open-ended questions may be too difficult for English-language learners to answer. If that is the case, ask closed questions such as "Can you put the fulcrum in the middle?" As you ask questions, use gestures to help children understand.

Read-Aloud

- Choose an alphabet book from the "Children's Books" list found on pages 109–118. See the accompanying guidance for sharing the book with children.

English-Language Learners
Consider making alphabet books or labeling objects in all the languages spoken in your class. This will make the children feel welcome, help them think about the vocabulary, and promote literacy.

Small-Group

Option 1: Asking Questions

- Review *Intentional Teaching Card* LL54, "Asking Questions." Follow the guidance on the card.

Option 2: That's How You Do It!

- Review *Intentional Teaching Card* LL78, "That's How You Do It!" Follow the guidance on the card to make a how-to chart for making different kinds of levers.

Mighty Minutes®

- Use *Mighty Minutes* 153, "Washing Machine." Follow the guidance on the card.

Large-Group Roundup

- Recall the day's events.
- Invite the children who experimented with balance levers in the Discovery area to share their observations.

How are levers used?

Vocabulary

English: *tools*; See *Book Discussion Card 56, Owen,* for additional words.

Spanish: *herramientas*

Question of the Day: Can you tear the paper on this line? (Provide a piece of paper with a straight line down the middle.)

Large Group

Opening Routine:

- Sing a welcome song and talk about who's here.

Game: 1, 2, 3, What Do I See?

- Use *Mighty Minutes* 50, "1, 2, 3, What Do I See?" Follow the guidance on the back of the card to play the game by placing several items related to levers throughout the classroom.

Discussion and Shared Writing: Paper and Levers

- Review the question of the day and invite the children to share the paper they tore along the line.

- Ask, "What *tool* could help us cut the paper along the line?" Explain that a *tool* is something that "makes it easier to do work."

- Record the children's answers on a sheet of chart paper.

- Show the children a pair of scissors. Explain that scissors are two levers working together.

- Point to the blades and the fulcrum of the scissors and discuss the parts.

- Model how to hold and use the scissors to cut the paper.

- Invite the children to take turns using scissors to cut paper.

Before transitioning to interest areas, point out the levers that are available in the Art area for the children to cut or work with paper.

Choice Time

As you interact with children in the interest areas, make time to do the following:

- Observe how the children are using the scissors, hole punchers, or staplers to work with paper.

- Talk about each tool with the children. Ask them to point out the planes and the fulcrum of each lever.

- Ask open-ended questions to encourage the children to think about how each tool is a lever such as, "Where is the fulcrum on these scissors?"

For more information about supporting children as they cut with scissors, see *Intentional Teaching Card* P08, "Cutting With Scissors."

Read-Aloud

Read *Owen*.

- Use *Book Discussion Card* 56, *Owen*.
  Follow the guidance for the second
  read-aloud.

Small-Group

Option 1: Patterns

- Review *Intentional Teaching Card* M14,
  "Patterns." Follow the guidance on
  the card.

Option 2: Picture Patterns

- Review *Intentional Teaching Card* M45,
  "Picture Patterns." Follow the guidance
  on the card.

Mighty Minutes®

- Use *Mighty Minutes* 31, "What's
  Inside the Box?" Follow the guidance
  on the card.

Large-Group Roundup

- Recall the day's events.
- Invite the children who worked with the
  scissors, hole punchers, and staplers in
  the Art area to share their work.

How do screws hold things together?

Vocabulary—English: *nut, bolt, screw, nail, threads, pitch, rotate,* words related to tools and equipment at a tire shop (e.g., lift, wrench, lug nut), *screw drive,* words related to types of screwdrivers (e.g., Phillips, Allen, slotted), *diameter*

	Day 1	Day 2	Day 3
Interest Areas	**Toys and Games:** sections of pegboard; screws; nuts and bolts	**Toys and Games:** screws; nails; 1-inch sections of pool noodles cut in half lengthwise	**Dramatic Play:** materials to create a tire shop; photos from the tire shop visit
Question of the Day	How can you hold these things together? (Display two pieces of pegboard.)	Is this a screw? (Display a nail.)	What do you want to find out on our site visit?
Large Group	**Game:** Crazy Compounds **Discussion and Shared Writing:** Exploring Screws **Materials:** *Mighty Minutes* 198, "Crazy Compounds"; screws; nuts; bolts; nails; chart paper	**Rhyme:** Ticky Ricky **Discussion and Shared Writing:** Why Do Screws Have Threads? **Materials:** *Mighty Minutes* 12, "Ticky Ricky"; chart paper; screws; paper; crayons	**Song:** "Dinky Doo" **Discussion and Shared Writing:** Site Visit to a Tire Shop **Materials:** *Mighty Minutes* 24, "Dinky Doo"; chart paper; clipboards; paper; pencils; camera
Read-Aloud	*Highlights High Five Bilingüe*™, *¡Para ti!/For You!* *Book Conversation Card* 02	*Owen* *Book Discussion Card* 56 (third read-aloud)	Nonfiction book from the "Children's Books" list
Small Group	**Option 1: Straw Shapes** *Intentional Teaching Card* M42, "Straw Shapes"; geometric shapes; drinking straws cut to different lengths; pipe cleaners; paper; pencil or crayons **Option 2: The Farmer Builds a Fence** *Intentional Teaching Card* M50, "The Farmer Builds a Fence"; elastic band or rope (about 8 feet long) with ends attached; two-dimensional shapes	**Option 1: Alphabet Books** *Intentional Teaching Card* LL34, "Alphabet Books"; books about the alphabet; construction paper; markers; alphabet cards **Option 2: Jumping Beans** *Intentional Teaching Card* LL05, "Jumping Beans"; construction paper; marker; scissors; lamination supplies or clear contact paper; coffee can	**Option 1: My Shadow and I** *Intentional Teaching Card* M47, "My Shadow and I"; overhead projector or flashlights; construction paper or colored transparencies; shapes **Option 2: Geoboards** *Intentional Teaching Card* M21, "Geoboards"; geoboards; geobands; shape cards with one shape on each card
Mighty Minutes®	*Mighty Minutes* 48, "Feely Box"	*Mighty Minutes* 178, "Happy Moths"	*Mighty Minutes* 156, "This Long Road"

Spanish: *tuerca, perno, tornillo, clavo, rosca, paso, rotar,* palabras relacionadas con herramientas y equipo en una tienda de neumáticos, *cabeza del tornillo,* palabras relacionadas con tipos de destornilladores (e.g., punta plana, estrella, hexagonal), *diámetro*

Day 4	Day 5	Make Time for…
Art: woodworking materials including screws and screwdrivers	**Toys and Games:** collection of screw-top bottles and caps	**Outdoor Experiences** • Bring screw top jars and containers outdoors.
What comes next in the pattern? (Stamp different screw heads into molding dough or clay.)	Can you open and close these bottles?	**Physical Fun** • Review *Intentional Teaching Card* P43, "Box Dribble," and *Intentional Teaching Card* P18, "Dribbling a Ball." Follow the guidance on the card.
Song: "Wind-Up Robots" **Discussion and Shared Writing:** Heads of Screws **Materials:** *Mighty Minutes* 194, "Wind-Up Robots"; screws with a variety of heads; chart paper	**Song:** "We Like Clapping" **Discussion and Shared Writing:** Screw Top Bottles **Materials:** *Mighty Minutes* 89, "We Like Clapping"; screw-top bottles; chart paper	**Family Partnerships** • Invite families to contribute clean screw-top bottles and jars. • Invite families to accompany children on the site visit to a local tire shop (Day 3).
Lola Loves Stories	Fiction book from the "Children's Books" list	**Wow! Experiences** • Day 3: Site visit to a local tire shop to see how screws are used
Option 1: Bigger Than, Smaller Than, Equal To *Intentional Teaching Card* M09, "Bigger Than, Smaller Than, Equal To"; building blocks or other stackable items; standard and nonstandard measuring tools; plastic links or yarn **Option 2: Pendulum Power** *Intentional Teaching Card* M83, "Pendulum Power"; nylon stockings; tennis balls; blocks; small cardboard boxes; collection of cardboard tubes; two chairs; broom or mop	**Option 1: What's for Snack?** *Intentional Teaching Card* LL25, "What's for Snack?"; food product labels, large paper or tagboard, marker, recipe cards or charts **Option 2: Roll-Ups** *Intentional Teaching Card* LL37, "Roll-Ups"; ingredients; chart paper and marker; plastic knives	
Mighty Minutes 100, "La, La, La"	*Mighty Minutes* 33, "Thumbs Up"	

How do screws hold things together?

Vocabulary

English: *nut, bolt, screw, nail*

Spanish: *tuerca, perno, tornillo, clavo*

Question of the Day: How can you hold these things together? (Display two pieces of pegboard.)

Large Group

Opening Routine:

- Sing a welcome song and talk about who's here.

Game: Crazy Compounds

- Use *Mighty Minutes* 198, "Crazy Compounds." Follow the guidance on the card.

Discussion and Shared Writing: Exploring Screws

- Show the children screws, nut and bolts, and nails. Remind the children that a *screw* is "a type of simple machine."

- Explain that *screws*, *nuts and bolts*, and *nails* are all materials that are "used to hold things together," but they work in different ways.

- Create a chart with three columns labeled "Screws," "Nuts & Bolts," and "Nails."

- Ask, "What do you notice about the characteristics of these items?" Record the children's responses on the appropriate column of the chart.

- Review the chart you created together and point out the differences between screws, nut and bolts, and nails.

Before transitioning to interest areas, point out the sections of pegboard, screws, and nuts and bolts that are available in the Toys and Games area and talk about how the children can use them.

Choice Time

As you interact with children in the interest areas, make time to do the following:

- Review the question of the day and invite the children to join the pieces of pegboard together using different materials.

- Model how to use the screws and nuts and bolts to join pieces of pegboard together.

- Ask questions and encourage the children to compare how screws and nuts and bolts are used differently.

Read-Aloud

Read *Highlights High Five Bilingüe*™, *¡Para ti!/For You!*

- Choose a few literacy experiences to share with children.

- Use *Book Conversation Card* 02, *¡Para ti!/For You!* Follow the guidance on the card.

Small-Group

Option 1: Straw Shapes

- Review *Intentional Teaching Card* M42, "Straw Shapes." Follow the guidance on the card.

Option 2: The Farmer Builds a Fence

- Review *Intentional Teaching Card* M50, "The Farmer Builds a Fence." Follow the guidance on the card.

Mighty Minutes®

- Use *Mighty Minutes* 48, "Feely Box." Follow the guidance on the back of the card using items from the study.

Large-Group Roundup

- Recall the day's events.
- Invite the children who used the screws and nuts and bolts in the Toys and Games area to share their observations.

How do screws hold things together?

Vocabulary

English: *threads, pitch;* See *Book Discussion Card 56, Owen,* for additional words.

Spanish: *rosca, paso*

Question of the Day: Is this a screw? (Display a nail.)

Large Group

Opening Routine:

- Sing a welcome song and talk about who's here.

Rhyme: Ticky Ricky

- Use *Mighty Minutes* 12, "Ticky Ricky." Follow the guidance on the card using items from the study.

Discussion and Shared Writing: Why Do Screws Have Threads?

- Review the question of the day. Ask, "How do you know the nail is not a screw?"

- Introduce the word *thread*. Explain that the *thread* of a screw is "the raised line that wraps around the screw."

- Ask, "Why do you think screws have threads?" Record the children's answers.

- Display or pass around screws that have different diameters and *pitches*. Explain that *pitch* means "the amount of space between the threads."

- Give the children a few minutes to examine and compare the screws.

- Provide the children with paper and crayons, markers, or colored pencils and invite them to make an observational drawing of the screw.

- After several minutes, invite the children to share their drawings and talk about their observations. Document what the children say about their drawings.

Before transitioning to interest areas, point out the screws and nails that are available in the Toys and Games area and talk about how the children can use them.

Choice Time

As you interact with children in the interest areas, make time to do the following:

- Demonstrate how to push or twist the screws and nails into the sections of pool noodle.

- Talk with the children about what they observe while using the materials such as "It's hard to push the bolt in because it doesn't have a pointy end," or "Screws work better when you turn them one way than the other way."

- Record the children's observations.

- Repeat the question "Why do screws have threads?" and continue to record the children's observations.

Read-Aloud

Read *Owen*.

- Use Book Discussion Card 56, *Owen*. Follow the guidance for the third read-aloud.

Small-Group

Option 1: Alphabet Books

- Review *Intentional Teaching Card* LL34, "Alphabet Books." Follow the guidance on the card using words related to the study.

Option 2: Jumping Beans

- Review *Intentional Teaching Card* LL05, "Jumping Beans." Follow the guidance on the card.

Mighty Minutes®

- Use *Mighty Minutes* 178, "Happy Moths." Follow the guidance on the card.

Large-Group Roundup

- Recall the day's events.
- Invite children who worked with the screws and nails to share their observations.
- Review the "Why do screws have threads?" chart and share the observations the children made in the Toys and Games area.
- Explain that tomorrow you will be visiting a tire shop to see how screws are used there.

How do screws hold things together?

Vocabulary

English: words related to tools and equipment at a tire shop

Spanish: palabras relacionadas con herramientas y equipo en una tienda de neumáticos

Question of the Day: What do you want to find out on our site visit?

Large Group

Opening Routine:

- Sing a welcome song and talk about who's here.

Sing: Dinky Doo

- Use *Mighty Minutes* 24, "Dinky Doo." Follow the guidance on the card.

Discussion and Shared Writing: Site Visit to a Tire Shop

- Review the question of the day. Invite the children to share what they would like to find out on the site visit. Document their questions.

> **Remind children about the expectations for the site visit. See *Intentional Teaching Card* SE01, "Site Visit," for more information.**

- Before the site visit, provide each child with a clipboard and pencil to use to record their observations at the tire shop.

- While on the visit, invite the children to ask their questions and record the responses.

- Ask the workers to share how they use screws or bolts to secure tires and what tools they use to loosen and tighten them.

- As the children observe, introduce words related to the tools or actions they see.

- Point out the threads on the screws and discuss the pitch.

- While at the tire shop, encourage the children to look for other simple machines that are used as well such as levers and inclined planes.

- Take photos to refer to later as the children set up their own tire shop in the Dramatic Play area.

Before transitioning to interest areas, talk with the children about the materials that are available in the Dramatic Play area. Discuss how the children can use the materials to set up their own tire shop.

Choice Time

As you interact with children in the interest areas, make time to do the following:

- Observe how children work cooperatively to create a tire shop in the Dramatic Play area.

- Encourage children to refer to their observational drawings as well as photos taken from the site visit to the tire shop.

- Ask children for suggestions of tools and materials they need for their tire shop. Document their suggestions on a list.

Continue the tire shop in the Dramatic Play area throughout the study. Update and add materials to the area that the children suggest.

Read-Aloud

- Choose a nonfiction book from the "Children's Books" list found on pages 109–118. See the accompanying guidance for sharing the book with children.

Small-Group

Option 1: My Shadow and I

- Review *Intentional Teaching Card* M47, "My Shadow and I." Follow the guidance on the card.

Option 2: Geoboards

- Review *Intentional Teaching Card* M21, "Geoboards." Follow the guidance on the card.

Mighty Minutes®

- Use *Mighty Minutes* 156, "This Long Road." Follow the guidance on the card.

Large-Group Roundup

- Recall the day's events.

- Invite the children who began setting up the tire shop to share their work.

- Review the list of materials the children suggested for the tire shop. Invite them to add more ideas to the list.

How do screws hold things together?

Vocabulary

English: *screw drive, rotate,* words related to types of screwdrivers such as Phillips, Allen, or slotted

Spanish: *cabeza del tornillo, rotar,* palabras relacionadas con tipos de destornilladores tales como *punta plana, estrella o hexagonal*

Question of the Day: What comes next in the pattern? (Stamp different screw heads into molding dough or clay.)

Large Group

Opening Routine:

- Sing a welcome song and talk about who's here.

Song: "Wind-Up Robots"

- Use *Mighty Minutes* 194, "Wind-Up Robots." Follow the guidance on the card.

Discussion and Shared Writing: Heads of Screws

- Review the question of the day. Point out how the different screw heads make different impressions in the clay. Explain that the head of a screw is called a *screw drive.*

- Display or pass around screws with different types of heads such as Phillips, Allen, or slotted.

- Give the children a few minutes to compare the screw heads and then ask, "What do you notice is different about the screw drives on these screws?" Document the children's answers on a sheet of chart paper.

- Give the children the name for each type of screw drive that was shown.

- Say, "There are special tools that fit into each of these screw drives that help you turn or *rotate* the screw."

- Pass out different kinds of screwdrivers or wrenches. Invite the children to find the corresponding tool for each screw.

Before transitioning to interest areas, point out the tools and screws that are available for the children in the Art area.

Choice Time

As you interact with children in the interest areas, make time to do the following:

- Observe how the children use the screws and screwdrivers in the Art area.

- Ask, "How did you decide which tool would work best for your screw?"

- Encourage the children to notice which way the screws need to rotate to go in and which way they need to rotate them to take them out.

Read-Aloud

- Read *Lola Loves Stories* from the "Children's Books" list found on pages 109–118. See the accompanying guidance for sharing the book with children.

Small-Group

Option 1: Bigger Than, Smaller Than, Equal To

- Review *Intentional Teaching Card* M09, "Bigger Than, Smaller Than, Equal To." Follow the guidance on the card.

Option 2: Pendulum Power

- Review *Intentional Teaching Card* M83, "Pendulum Power." Follow the guidance on the card.

Mighty Minutes®

- Use *Mighty Minutes* 100, "La, La, La." Follow the guidance on the card.

Large-Group Roundup

- Recall the day's events.
- Invite the children who worked with the tools and screws in the Art area to share their observations.
- Invite children to bring in plastic screw-top bottles such as water or juice containers from home.

How do screws hold things together?

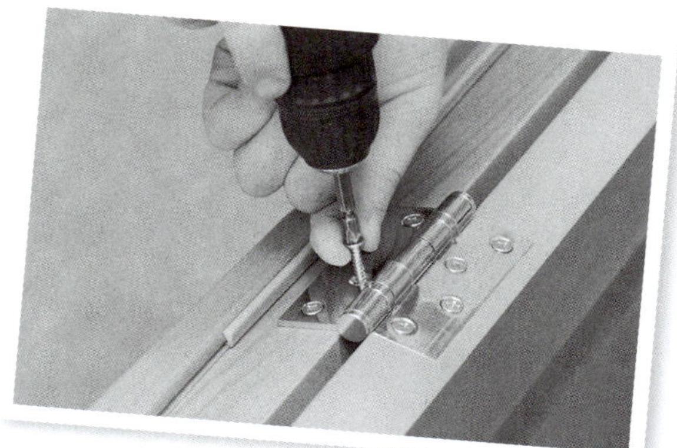

Vocabulary

English: *diameter*
Spanish: *diámetro*
Question of the Day: Can you open and close these bottles?

Large Group

Opening Routine:

- Sing a welcome song and talk about who's here.

Song: "We Like Clapping"

- Use *Mighty Minutes* 89, "We Like Clapping." Follow the guidance on the back of the card, incorporating the children's ideas to vary the movements.

Discussion and Shared Writing: Screw Top Bottles

- Display a collection of screw-top bottles. Invite the children to share the bottles they brought from home.

- Review the question of the day. Pass around the bottles and encourage the children to twist open and close the caps.

- Explain that the top of the bottle is a screw and point out the threads that are on the top of the bottle and inside the cap.

- When each child has a bottle, collect all of the caps and place them in a pile in the middle or front of the group.

- Invite the children to take turns finding the cap that matches their bottle.

- Ask, "How did you know which cap belonged with your bottle?" Record the children's answers on a sheet of chart paper.

> **See *Intentional Teaching Card* M58, "Missing Lids,"** for more guidance on supporting children as they match the caps to the bottles.

English-Language Learners
If possible, include containers that have environmental print in children's home languages. Having environmental print in home languages helps all children participate and feel proud of their cultures and families.

Before transitioning to interest areas, tell the children that the bottles and caps will be available in the Toys and Games area so that they can continue to explore them.

Choice Time

As you interact with children in the interest areas, make time to do the following:

- Talk with the children about the differences between the screw tops. Introduce the word *diameter*. Explain that the *diameter* means "how wide a circle is" like the opening of the bottle or the cap of the bottle.

- Encourage the children to notice which way they need to twist the cap to put it on the bottle and which way they turn it to take it off of the bottle.

- Point out the threads on the top of the bottle and count them with the children.

- Encourage the children to compare how many turns it takes to remove the cap from the bottle with how many threads the top has. For example, you could say, "This top has eight threads; how many turns do you think it will take to take it off?"

- Invite the children to continue counting the turns for other screw-top lids and predicting how many turns it will take to take them off.

> **Some screw-top bottles have one thread while others may have two. You can determine this by looking at the top of the threads and seeing how many starting points there are. Use bottles that only have one thread to make it easier for the children to predict the number of turns.**

> **Place a mark on the edge of the bottle cap and side of the bottle to make it easier to count each rotation.**

Read-Aloud

- Choose a fiction book from the "Children's Books" list found on pages 109–118. See the accompanying guidance for sharing the book with children.

Small-Group

Option 1: What's for Snack?

- Review *Intentional Teaching Card* LL25, "What's for Snack?" Follow the guidance on the card.

Option 2: Roll-Ups

- Review *Intentional Teaching Card* LL37, "Roll-Ups." Follow the guidance on the card.

Mighty Minutes®

- Use *Mighty Minutes* 33, "Thumbs Up." Follow the guidance on the card.

Large-Group Roundup

- Recall the day's events.

- Invite the children who matched the screw-top bottles and caps in the Toys and Games area to share their observations.

- Give each child a screw-top bottle with its cap on. Ask, "Which way do you turn the cap to take it off?" Give the children time to experiment turning the cap each way.

Investigation 4

What are other types of simple machines?

Vocabulary—English: *cable, pulley, blade, wedge, skate, energy*

	Day 1	Day 2
Interest Areas	**Blocks:** pulley	**Cooking:** ingredients and cooking tools
Question of the Day	What shape is this? (Display a wheel of a pulley.)	Is this a simple machine? (Show an image of a kitchen knife.)
Large Group	**Game:** Come Play With Me **Discussion and Shared Writing:** Exploring Pulleys **Materials:** *Mighty Minutes* 42, "Come Play With Me"; pictures of pulleys; chart paper; pulley	**Song:** "Two Plump Armadillos" **Discussion and Shared Writing:** Visitor Who Uses Wedges in the Kitchen **Materials:** *Mighty Minutes* 44, "Two Plump Armadillos"; chart paper
Read-Aloud	*My Neighbors and Their Simple Machines*	*Featherless* *Book Discussion Card* 58 (first read-aloud)
Small Group	**Option 1: Alphabet Cards** *Intentional Teaching Card* LL03, "Alphabet Cards"; 52 large cards; small manipulatives **Option 2: Textured Letters** *Intentional Teaching Card* LL15, "Textured Letters"; uppercase and lowercase letters cut out of a variety of materials; heavy paper or card stock	**Option 1: Play Dough** *Intentional Teaching Card* M15, "Play Dough"; recipe chart; ingredients; measuring cups; spoons; circle cutters of various sizes; scoops; large resealable bags; measuring tools **Option 2: Biscuits** *Intentional Teaching Card* M10, "Biscuits"; recipe chart; ingredients; materials to make biscuits
Mighty Minutes®	*Mighty Minutes* 181, "Line Dancing"	*Mighty Minutes* 101, "I'm Sticky"

How do people use them?

Spanish: *cable, polea, filo, cuña, patín, energía*

Day 3	Day 4	Make Time for…
Toys and Games: roller skates; wheels; tools to change wheels	**Art:** photos of simple machines in the community; clay; tools to work with the clay	
How is this used? (Show an image of a roller skate.)	What will we see on our walk today?	
Movement: Counting Calisthenics **Discussion and Shared Writing:** Roller Skating Visitor **Materials:** *Mighty Minutes* 28, "Counting Calisthenics"; chart paper	**Game:** Number Lineup **Discussion and Shared Writing:** Simple Machines in Our Neighborhood **Materials:** *Mighty Minutes* 118, "Number Lineup"; clipboard; paper; pencils; chart paper	
Highlights High Five Bilingüe™, *¡Vamos a leer!/Let's Read!* *Book Conversation Card* 10	*Featherless* *Book Discussion Card* 58 (second read-aloud)	
Option 1: Stepping Stones *Intentional Teaching Card* M55, "Stepping Stones"; masking tape or chalk **Option 2: We're Going on an Adventure** *Intentional Teaching Card* M36, "We're Going on an Adventure"; materials to make an adventure course; photographs with geographic features	**Option 1: Writing Poems** *Intentional Teaching Card* LL27, "Writing Poems"; paper; pencils; markers; chart paper; audio recorder **Option 2: Simple Machines Poems** *Intentional Teaching Card* LL27, "Writing Poems"; collection of simple machines; paper; pencils; markers; chart paper; audio recorder	
Mighty Minutes 161, "Baxter the Black Dog"	*Mighty Minutes* 37, "Little Ball"	

Outdoor Experiences

- Create an outdoor pulley on a stable playground structure for the children to use.

Physical Fun

- Review *Intentional Teaching Card* P07, "Balloon Catch" and *Intentional Teaching Card* P06, "Catching With a Scoop." Follow the guidance on the card.

Family Partnerships

- Invite a family member who cooks to visit the classroom.
- Invite a family member who roller skates to visit the classroom

Wow! Experiences

- Day 2: Visit from a family member to talk about how he or she uses knives while cooking
- Day 3: Visit from a family member who roller skates
- Day 4: Take a walk to look for simple machines.
- Research local carpenters to invite to visit the classroom next week.
- Research bicycle shops for the children to visit next week.

Preparing for the Week: Construct a simple pulley system using a wall or other stable classroom structure. Place a basket or bucket at the end of the pulley to carry the load.

What are other types of simple machines? How do people use them?

Vocabulary

English: *cable, pulley*

Spanish: *cable, polea*

Question of the Day: What shape is this? (Display a wheel of a pulley.)

Large Group

Opening Routine:

- Sing a welcome song and talk about who's here.

Game: Come Play With Me

- Use *Mighty Minutes* 42, "Come Play With Me." Follow the guidance on the card.

Discussion and Shared Writing: Exploring Pulleys

- Review the question of the day and introduce the word *pulley*. Explain that a *pulley* is "something used to lift things and is made with a rope and a wheel."

- Show the children photos of pulleys being used. Pass the photos around and give the children a few minutes to look at the pictures.

- Ask, "What is a pulley used for?" Document the children's answers on a sheet of chart paper.

- Ask, "Why would you use a pulley to lift these things?" and continue to record the children's responses.

- Point to the pulley that you set up in the classroom. Demonstrate how to use the pulley by pulling the cord down to raise the basket.

- Ask the children to suggest different items they can lift with the pulley. Write the children's suggestions on a sheet of chart paper and post the chart near the pulley.

Before transitioning to interest areas, show the children the pulley that is set up in the Block area and talk with the children about how they can use it to lift and lower loads.

Choice Time

As you interact with children in the interest areas, make time to do the following:

- Observe how the children use the pulley to lift various items.

- Review the list of suggested items to lift with the pulley. Invite the children to load the items into the basket and lift them.

- Talk with the children about how the pulley helps to lift things.

- Ask open-ended questions to encourage the children to predict and compare how the pulley will help to lift the different items.

Read-Aloud

- Read *My Neighbors and Their Simple Machines*.

- Invite the children to recall any information they remember from the book.

Small-Group

Option 1: Alphabet Cards

- Review *Intentional Teaching Card* LL03, "Alphabet Cards." Follow the guidance on the card.

Option 2: Textured Letters

- Review *Intentional Teaching Card* LL15, "Textured Letters." Follow the guidance on the card.

Mighty Minutes®

- Use *Mighty Minutes* 181, "Line Dancing." Follow the guidance on the card.

Large-Group Roundup

- Recall the day's events.

- Invite the children who experimented with the pulley in the Block area to share their observations.

- Explain that tomorrow there will be a special visitor who is an expert at using a different type of simple machine in the kitchen.

- Ask, "What would you like to ask our visitor tomorrow?"

- Record the children's questions.

What are other types of simple machines? How do people use them?

Vocabulary

English: *blade, wedge;* See *Book Discussion Card 58, Featherless,* for additional words.

Spanish: *filo, cuña*

Question of the Day: Is this a simple machine? (Show an image of a kitchen knife.)

Large Group

Opening Routine:

- Sing a welcome song and talk about who's here.

Song: "Two Plump Armadillos"

- Use *Mighty Minutes* 44, "Two Plump Armadillos." Follow the guidance on the card.

Discussion and Shared Writing: Visitor Who Uses Wedges in the Kitchen

- Review the question of the day.

- Discuss that a knife is a type of simple machine called a *wedge*. Explain that a *wedge* is "a tool that has a point that is used to split something apart."

- Show and discuss pictures of different kinds of wedges being used such as an axe splitting wood or a knife cutting food.

- Introduce the visitor.

- Invite the visitor to talk about how he uses knives while cooking.

- Encourage the children to ask their questions from yesterday's large-group roundup. Record the responses.

- Ask, "What kinds of food are cut with a knife?" Record the children's answers and invite the visitor to talk about how each food is cut or prepared.

Before transitioning to interest areas, explain that there are ingredients in the Cooking area for the children to use to make fruit salad.

Choice Time

As you interact with children in the interest areas, make time to do the following:

> **Follow the guidance on *Intentional Teaching Card* LL35, "Fruit Salad," to set up the cooking experience.**

- Invite the visitor to model how to hold and use the knife to cut the fruit pieces.
- Provide plastic knives or butter knives for the children to use to cut the fruit.

- Observe how the children use their fingers and hands to hold and manipulate the knife.
- Talk with the children about how the *blade* of the knife is used to cut the food. Explain that the blade is the flat part of the knife that is used as a wedge.
- Invite the children to try cutting the fruit with different tools and comparing the results.

Read-Aloud

Read *Featherless*.

- Use *Book Discussion Card* 58, *Featherless*. Follow the guidance for the first read-aloud.

Small-Group

Option 1: Play Dough

- Review *Intentional Teaching Card* M15, "Play Dough." Follow the guidance on the card.
- After making the molding dough, provide the children with different wedge tools such as plastic knives, pizza cutters, or other cutters to use to cut the dough.

Option 2: Biscuits

- Review *Intentional Teaching Card* M10, "Biscuits." Follow the guidance on the card.
- Invite the children to cut the biscuits into shapes using a knife or another wedge tool such as a pizza cutter.

Mighty Minutes®

- Use *Mighty Minutes* 101, "I'm Sticky." Follow the guidance on the card.

Large-Group Roundup

- Recall the day's events.
- Invite the children who used different wedges to cut during small-group or choice time to share their experiences.
- Have the children help you create a thank-you card for the visitor. Invite children to sign their names and add drawings to the note.

- Explain that tomorrow someone who uses wheels and axles will be visiting the classroom.
- Help children generate questions to ask the visitor tomorrow. Record their questions on a sheet of chart paper.

What are other types of simple machines? How do people use them?

Vocabulary
English: *skate*
Spanish: *patín*
Question of the Day: How is this used? (Show an image of a roller skate.)

Large Group

Opening Routine:

- Sing a welcome song and talk about who's here.

Movement: Counting Calisthenics

- Use *Mighty Minutes* 28, "Counting Calisthenics." Follow the guidance on the back of the card, creating a four-step action as you count.

Discussion and Shared Writing: Roller Skating Visitor

- Review the question of the day. Explain that the picture is of a *skate*, which is "a boot that has wheels on the bottom."

- Ask, "Who have you seen use skates?" Record the children's answers on a sheet of chart paper.

- Introduce the visitor and ask her to explain how she uses skates.

- Ask the visitor to demonstrate different strides and steps she uses while skating. Encourage the children to perform the movements along with the visitor.

- Explain that skates use simple machines, including a wheel and axle and screws.

- Invite the visitor to show her skates and talk about what kinds of wheels are on them. Ask the visitor to demonstrate how to take off and put wheels onto the skate.

- As the visitor is changing the wheels on the skate, point out the parts of the wheel such as the axle it goes onto and the screw at the end of the axle that the nut fits onto to hold the wheel in place.

- Encourage the children to ask the visitor the questions they thought of at yesterday's large-group roundup. Record the responses.

- Invite the visitor to stay through choice time to give the children an opportunity to explore her skates and wheels.

English-Language Learners
When introducing new words such as *skate*, determine whether the English words are a new way of labeling a concept that English-language learners already know. If not, teach children both the concept (preferably in their home languages) and the new words.

Before transitioning to interest areas, explain that the children will have an opportunity to explore the wheels and axles of the visitor's roller skates in the Toys and Games area.

Choice Time

As you interact with children in the interest areas, make time to do the following:

- Ask the children to point out and identify the different simple machines that are on the skates.

- Invite the children to take turns using the tools to change the wheels on the skates.

- Encourage the children to ask the visitor questions as they examine the skates.

Read-Aloud

Read *Highlights High Five Bilingüe*™, *¡Vamos a leer!/Let's Read!*

- Choose a few literacy experiences to share with children.

- Use *Book Conversation Card* 06, *¡Vamos a leer!/Let's Read!* Follow the guidance on the card.

Small-Group

Option 1: Stepping Stones

- Review *Intentional Teaching Card* M55, "Stepping Stones." Follow the guidance on the card.

Option 2: We're Going on an Adventure

- Review *Intentional Teaching Card* M36, "We're Going on an Adventure." Follow the guidance on the card.

Mighty Minutes®

- Use *Mighty Minutes* 161, "Baxter the Black Dog." Follow the guidance on the card.

Large-Group Roundup

- Recall the day's events.

- Show the children a picture of a roller skate and invite them to point out the simple machines they found during choice time.

- Have the children help you create a thank-you card for the visitor. Invite children to sign their names and add drawings to the card.

What are other types of simple machines? How do people use them?

Vocabulary

English: *energy;* See *Book Discussion Card 58, Featherless,* for additional words.
Spanish: *energía*
Question of the Day: What will we see on our walk today?

Large Group

Opening Routine:

- Sing a welcome song and talk about who's here.

Game: Number Lineup

- Use *Mighty Minutes* 118, "Number Lineup." Follow the guidance on the card.

Discussion and Shared Writing: Simple Machines in Our Neighborhood

- Explain, "Now that we know about more types of simple machines, we will be taking a walk today to see what simple machines we notice in our neighborhood."

- Review the question of the day.

- Remind the children about the different types of simple machines you have investigated and give a few examples of where they might be found in the community. For example you may say, "Sometimes a pulley is used to raise and lower a flag on a flag pole. I am going to look at the flag pole in front of the building to see if there is a pulley."

- Give each child a clipboard and pencil to document what she sees while on the walk.

- When the children find a simple machine, give them enough time to document it on their paper.

- Talk about how the simple machine is used. Introduce the word *energy*. Explain that *energy* means "the power it takes to move" such as how you use your body when using a simple machine.

- After the walk, invite the children to share their observations.

- Ask, "What simple machines did you see on the walk?" Record the children's responses on a sheet of chart paper.

Before transitioning to interest areas, point out the photos of simple machines and clay in the Art area. Talk with the children about how they can use the clay to make simple machines

Choice Time

As you interact with children in the interest areas, make time to do the following:

- Observe how the children are using the clay to make simple machines. Describe what you see as they work.

- Ask open-ended questions to encourage them to think of new ways they can work with the clay. For example, you may ask, "How are you going to make the thread for your screw?"

- Prompt children to name the parts they create for each simple machine.

- Ask the children to identify and talk about the simple machine they make.

Read-Aloud

Read *Featherless*.

- Use *Book Discussion Card* 58, *Featherless*. Follow the guidance for the second read-aloud.

Small-Group

Option 1: Writing Poems

- Review *Intentional Teaching Card* LL27, "Writing Poems." Follow the guidance on the card.

Option 2: Simple Machines Poems

- Review *Intentional Teaching Card* LL27, "Writing Poems."

- Display a collection of simple machines.

- Follow the guidance on the card to talk about the simple machines and write a poem about them.

Mighty Minutes®

- Use *Mighty Minutes* 37, "Little Ball." Follow the guidance on the card.

Large-Group Roundup

- Recall the day's events.

- Invite the children to share their poems from small-group time and record their readings.

Who works with simple machines?

Vocabulary—English: *work, complex machines, mechanic, haul*

	Day 1	Day 2
Interest Areas	**Art:** woodworking materials	**Discovery:** a complex machine or electronic machine the children can take apart; tools; pictures of simple machines
Question of the Day	What would you like to ask the visitor?	What do these items have in common? (Show a picture of skates, a bicycle, and a slide.)
Large Group	**Song:** "This Old Man" **Discussion and Shared Writing:** Visitor Who is a Carpenter **Materials:** *Mighty Minutes* 96, "This Old Man"; chart paper	**Movement:** Silly Dance **Discussion and Shared Writing:** Complex Machines **Materials:** *Mighty Minutes* 106, "Silly Dance"; pictures of a skate, a bicycle, and a slide
Read-Aloud	Selection of a counting book from the "Children's Books" list	Selection from the "Children's Books" list that features people who work with simple machines
Small Group	**Option 1: Memory Games** *Intentional Teaching Card* LL08, "Memory Games"; a set of duplicate pictures or objects **Option 2: What's Missing?** *Intentional Teaching Card* LL18, "What's Missing?"; bag or box with a variety of objects related to the study topic; large piece of paper or cardboard	**Option 1: Did You Ever See …?** *Intentional Teaching Card* LL14, "Did You Ever See …?"; pictures of familiar animals **Option 2: Simple Machine Riddles** *Intentional Teaching Card* LL11, "Rhyming Riddles"; chart paper and markers; simple machines; props that rhyme with chosen simple machines
Mighty Minutes®	*Mighty Minutes* 186, "Stop & Go Colors"	*Mighty Minutes* 126, "This Way or That Way?"

Day 3	Day 4	Make Time for…
Dramatic Play: bicycle props to add to the tire shop	**Discovery:** moving equipment and boxes	
How many wheels are on this bike?	Which simple machine can lift this? (Display a heavy object such as a container of blocks.)	
Movement: Away I Go	**Rhyme:** Riddle Dee Dee	
Discussion and Shared Writing: Site Visit to a Bicycle Shop	**Discussion and Shared Writing:** Visitor Who is a Delivery Worker or Mover	
Materials: *Mighty Minutes* 138, "Away I Go"; chart paper; camera	**Materials:** *Mighty Minutes* 04, "Riddle Dee Dee"; pictures of movers or delivery workers; chart paper	
Featherless *Book Discussion Card* 58 (third read-aloud)	*Highlights High Five Bilingüe*™, *¡Vamos a leer!/Let's Read!* *Book Conversation Card* 10	
Option 1: Oobleck *Intentional Teaching Card* M66, "Oobleck"; chart paper and marker; ingredients; large bowl; measuring cups **Option 2: Bicycle Shop Hop** *Intentional Teaching Card* M91, "Number Line Hop"; masking tape or chalk; numeral cards 1–20	**Option 1: Character Feelings** *Intentional Teaching Card* SE05, "Character Feelings"; books in which the characters experience a range of emotions **Option 2: Where Are My Feelings?** *Intentional Teaching Card* SE33, "Where Are My Feelings?"	
Mighty Minutes 87, "One, Two, Buckle My Shoe"	*Mighty Minutes* 114, "Traffic Jam"	

Outdoor Experiences

Physical Fun

- Review *Intentional Teaching Card* P36, "Tape Trails." Follow the guidance on the card to create paths over paved areas on the playground. Invite the children to ride their tricycles along the path.

Family Partnerships

- Invite families to accompany the class on the site visit to a local bicycle shop.

- Invite a family member who is a delivery worker or mover to visit the class

- Invite families to attend the end-of-study celebration. Send them a letter that explains the event.

Wow! Experiences

- Day 1: Visit from a local carpenter to share how he uses simple machines

- Day 3: Site visit to a bicycle shop to see how simple machines work together

- Day 4: Visit from a mover or delivery worker

Who works with simple machines?

Vocabulary

English: *work*
Spanish: *trabajo*
Question of the Day: What would you like to ask the visitor?

Large Group

Opening Routine:

- Sing a welcome song and talk about who's here.

Song: "This Old Man"

- Use *Mighty Minutes* 96, "This Old Man." Follow the guidance on the back of the card to march, dance, or move together as you sing the song.

Discussion and Shared Writing: Visitor Who is a Carpenter

- Introduce the visitor.

- Invite the visitor to explain his job and display some of the tools that are used.

- Ask, "What simple machines do you notice?" Record the children's responses on a sheet of chart paper.

- Review the question of the day and invite the children to ask the carpenter their questions.

- Invite the visitor to demonstrate how to use the tools that he brought.

- Explain that *work* is a word that means "the amount of effort it takes to do something" and that simple machines make *work* easier.

- Ask the carpenter to share how each tool makes *work* easier.

Before transitioning to interest areas, talk with the children about the carpenter tools that are available in the Art area for the children to use.

Choice Time

As you interact with children in the interest areas, make time to do the following:

- Observe how the children are using the woodworking tools.

- Point out the simple machines that you notice the children using.

- Ask questions such as "How is that tool helping you?" or "I see that you have a hammer; what can you use that for?"

- Take photos as the children work.

Read-Aloud

- Choose a counting book from the "Children's Books" list found on pages 109–118. See the accompanying guidance for ideas on sharing the book with children.

Small-Group

Option 1: Memory Games

- Review *Intentional Teaching Card* LL08, "Memory Games." Follow the guidance on the card.

Option 2: What's Missing?

- Review *Intentional Teaching Card* LL18, "What's Missing?"
- Follow the guidance on the card using simple machines as the objects.
- If the children cannot recall which item is missing, give them clues about how the missing simple machine works or what it is used for to help them remember.

Mighty Minutes®

- Use *Mighty Minutes* 186, "Stop & Go Colors." Follow the guidance on the card.

Large-Group Roundup

- Recall the day's events.
- Invite the children who used the carpenter tools in the Art area to share their work.

- Have the children help you create a thank-you card to the visitor. Invite children to sign their names and add drawings to the card.

Who works with simple machines?

Vocabulary

English: *complex machine*

Spanish: *máquina compuesta*

Question of the Day: What do these items have in common? (Show a picture of skates, a bicycle, and a slide.)

Large Group

Opening Routine:

- Sing a welcome song and talk about who's here.

Movement: Silly Dance

- Use *Mighty Minutes* 106, "Silly Dance." Follow the guidance on the card.

Discussion and Shared Writing: Complex Machines

- Review the question of the day. Explain that skates and bicycles both contain simple machines.

- Show the children the pictures from the question of the day and ask, "What simple machines do you see in the pictures?" Remind the children of the simple machines that you have investigated throughout the study.

- Record the children's responses by labeling the pictures.

- Once the pictures are labeled, introduce the term *complex machine*. Explain that a *complex machine* is "more than one simple machine working together."

- Explain that simple machines are often parts of other machines or devices.

Before transitioning to interest areas, talk with the children about the machine that is available in the Discovery area. Explain that they can use the tools to take the machine apart and look for simple machines.

Choice Time

As you interact with children in the interest areas, make time to do the following:

- Observe how they use the tools to take apart the machine in the Discovery area.

- Notice how the children are using their fingers and hands to use the tools and take apart the machine.

- As the children explore, ask open-ended questions to prompt them to think about the different types of simple machines they can find. For example, you may ask, "What kinds of levers can you find in this machine?"

Read-Aloud

- Choose a book from the "Children's Books" list on pages 109–118 that features people whose jobs involve simple machines.

Small-Group

Option 1: Did You Ever See …?

- Review *Intentional Teaching Card* LL14, "Did You Ever See …?" Follow the guidance on the card.

Option 2: Simple Machine Riddles

- Review *Intentional Teaching Card* LL11, "Rhyming Riddles."
- Follow the guidance on the card to create riddles about different simple machines using vocabulary words learned during the study.

Mighty Minutes®

- Use *Mighty Minutes* 126, "This Way or That Way?" Follow the guidance on the card.

Large-Group Roundup

- Recall the day's events.
- Invite the children who took apart the machine in the Discovery area to share which simple machines they found.
- Explain that tomorrow you will be visiting a bicycle shop to discover how simple machines work together on a bicycle.

- Ask, "What would you like to find out during the site visit tomorrow?" Record the children's answers on a sheet of chart paper.

Who works with simple machines?

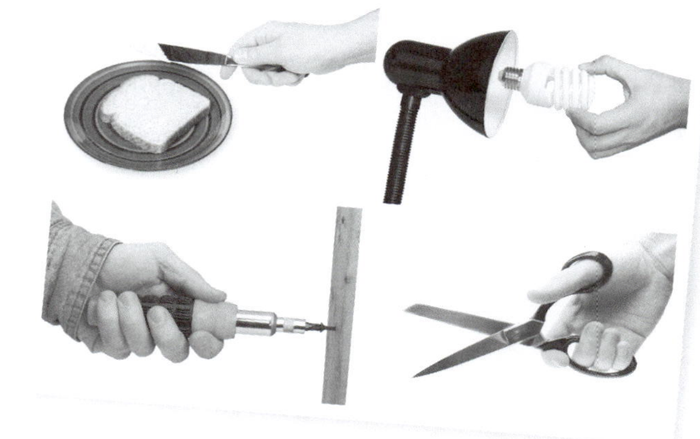

Vocabulary

English: *mechanic;* See *Book Discussion Card 58, Featherless,* for additional words.

Spanish: *mecánico*

Question of the Day: How many wheels are on this bike?

Large Group

Opening Routine:

- Sing a welcome song and talk about who's here.

Movement: Away I Go

- Use *Mighty Minutes* 138, "Away I Go." Follow the guidance on the card.

- Include one verse about a "bicycle pedaling down the path."

Discussion and Shared Writing: Site Visit to a Bicycle Shop

- Review the question of the day. Ask, "Do you think we will see bikes like this at the bicycle shop?"

- Ask, "What else do you think we will see?" Record the children's answers.

- Introduce the *mechanic* at the bicycle shop. Explain that a *mechanic* is "someone who fixes bikes or cars."

- Invite the mechanic to explain her job and show the children the bicycles she is working on.

- Point out the various simple machines that are on the bicycle and ask the children to identify them.

- Encourage the children to ask the mechanic their questions from yesterday's large-group roundup.

- Ask the mechanic mathematical questions about the bicycles that you see in the shop such as "How many bikes can you repair each day?" or "Do some bikes have different amounts of wheels?" or "How many gears does this bike have?" Record her responses to review later.

- Take photos of the site visit for the children to refer to later.

Before transitioning to interest areas, show the children photos from the site visit and talk about how they can incorporate ideas from the bike shop into their tire shop in the Dramatic Play area. Make a list of the materials they suggest to add to the Dramatic Play area.

Choice Time

As you interact with children in the interest areas, make time to do the following:

- Display photos from the site visit for the children to refer to and invite the children to continue to add materials they would like to add to the Dramatic Play area to the list.

- Support the children to collect materials from the list from around the classroom or the simple machines collection.

- Invite the children to compare what kinds of tools and simple machines were used at the tire shop and the bicycle shop.

Read-Aloud

Read *Featherless*.

- Use *Book Discussion Card* 58, *Featherless.* Follow the guidance for the third read-aloud.

Small-Group

Option 1: Oobleck

- Review *Intentional Teaching Card* M66, "Oobleck." Follow the guidance on the card.

Option 2: Bicycle Shop Hop

- Review *Intentional Teaching Card* M91, "Number Line Hop." Follow the guidance on the card and use the mathematical information that was gathered during the site visit. For example, the number of wheels on different bicycles that you saw, the number of bicycles the mechanic repairs in one day, the number of gears a bicycle has.

Mighty Minutes®

- Use *Mighty Minutes* 87, "One, Two, Buckle My Shoe." Follow the guidance on the card.

Large-Group Roundup

- Recall the day's events.
- Talk about the site visit and have the children help you create a thank-you card to the mechanic that you visited at the bicycle shop. Invite children to sign their names and add drawings to the card.

- Explain that tomorrow you will have a special visitor who is an expert at using simple machines to move heavy things.
- Ask, "What would you like to ask the visitor?" Record the children's answers on a sheet of chart paper.

Day 4 — Investigation 5

Who works with simple machines?

Vocabulary

English: *haul*

Spanish: *tirar o arrastrar*

Question of the Day: Which simple machine can lift this? (Display a heavy object such as a container of blocks.)

Large Group

Opening Routine:

- Sing a welcome song and talk about who's here.

Rhyme: Riddle Dee Dee

- Use *Mighty Minutes* 04, "Riddle Dee Dee." Follow the guidance on the card.

Discussion and Shared Writing: Visitor Who is a Delivery Worker or Mover

- Show the children pictures of movers or delivery workers working.

- Ask, "How do simple machines help them move heavy things?" Record the children's responses on a sheet of chart paper.

- Introduce the visitor to the children.

- Invite the visitor to share how he uses simple machines to move heavy things.

- Introduce the word *haul* into the conversation. Explain that *haul* is "another word for carry."

- Ask the visitor to share tools or pictures of the tools that he uses such as a ramp or a hand truck.

- Review the question of the day. Encourage the children and the visitor to discuss which simple machine would work best to lift the object.

Before transitioning to interest areas, explain that the children can explore moving equipment and experiment with moving boxes in the Discovery area.

Choice Time

As you interact with children in the interest areas, make time to do the following:

- Observe the children as they explore the moving equipment and boxes in the Discovery area.

- Ask open-ended questions to help the children think of different ways to use the moving equipment to move the boxes, such as "What do you think you can use to move two boxes at the same time?"

- Encourage the children to experiment with different-sized and weighted boxes.

- Ask the children to name the simple machines they are using and talk about how they help move the boxes.

Read-Aloud

Read Highlights High Five Bilingüe™, ¡Vamos a leer!/Let's Read!.

- Choose a few literacy experiences to share with children.

- Use *Book Conversation Card* 06, *¡Vamos a leer!/Let's Read!*. Follow the guidance on the card.

Small-Group

Option 1: Character Feelings

- Review *Intentional Teaching Card* SE05, "Character Feelings." Follow the guidance on the card.

Option 2: Where Are My Feelings?

- Review *Intentional Teaching Card* SE33, "Where Are My Feelings?" Follow the guidance on the card.

Mighty Minutes®

- Use *Mighty Minutes* 114, "Traffic Jam." Follow the guidance on the card.

Large-Group Roundup

- Recall the day's events.

- Invite the children who explored the moving equipment and boxes in the Discovery area to share their observations.

- With the children, write a thank-you note for the visitor. Invite the children to draw a picture and write their names on the note.

Additional Questions to Investigate

How can we extend this study further?

If children are still engaged in this study and want to find out more, you might want to investigate additional questions.

Here are some suggestions:

- How can we build a complex machine?
- What are the biggest and smallest simple machines?
- How do you decide which type of simple machines to use?
- What are other kinds of wedges and how are they used?
- How can we make it easier to lift items with a pulley?
- How do adults and children use simple machines differently?
- Did people use simple machines a long time ago?
- How do large drills make holes and tunnels?

Are there additional questions that will help you extend this study?

Our Investigation

Our Investigation

	Day 1	Day 2	Day 3
Interest Areas			
Question of the Day			
Large Group			
Read-Aloud			
Small Group			
Mighty Minutes®			

Day 4	Day 5	Make Time for…
		Outdoor Experiences
		Family Partnerships
		Wow! Experiences

Our Investigation

Vocabulary

English:

Spanish:

Question of the Day:

Large Group

Choice Time

Read-Aloud

Small-Group

Mighty Minutes®

Large-Group
Roundup

Our Investigation

Vocabulary

English:

Spanish:

Question of the Day:

Large Group

Choice Time

Read-Aloud

Small-Group

Mighty Minutes®

Large-Group Roundup

Our Investigation

Vocabulary

English:

Spanish:

Question of the Day:

Large Group

Choice Time

Read-Aloud

Small-Group

Mighty Minutes®

Large-Group
Roundup

Celebrating Learning

Closing the Study

When the study ends—when most of the children's questions have been answered—it is important to reflect and celebrate. Plan a special way to celebrate their learning and accomplishments. Encourage children to assume as much responsibility as possible for planning the activities. Here are some suggestions:

- Set up stations in the interest areas where children can show visitors how they investigated simple machines.

- Make a video of the class working with simple machines throughout the study for families to keep and enjoy at home.

- Set up stations with different scenarios such as, "How can we hold open the door?", "How can we lift the box?", or "How can we fix the toy?" Invite the children and the guests to test different simple machines to see which one works best to solve the problem.

- Invite children and guests to make their own complex machines by combining simple machines together.

- Create a class book, photo album, documentation panel, or slide show about the study.

The following pages provide daily plans for two days of celebration. Add your ideas and children's ideas for how to best celebrate all of their learning.

Celebrating Learning

Vocabulary—English: *celebrate* **Spanish:** *celebrar*

	Day 1	Day 2
Interest Areas	**All:** displays of the children's investigations	**All:** displays of the children's investigations **Blocks:** inclined planes and pulleys **Dramatic Play:** tire and bicycle shop materials **Library:** books you have read during the investigations **Toys and Games:** screws, nails, screw-top bottles **Discovery:** tools to use with simple machines
Question of the Day	What would you like to show our guests tomorrow at the celebration?	What was your favorite part of the study?
Large Group	**Game:** Sorting Syllables **Discussion and Shared Writing:** Planning the Celebration **Materials:** *Mighty Minutes* 95, "Sorting Syllables"; chart paper	**Song:** "Hello, How Are You?" **Discussion and Shared Writing:** Sharing Simple Machines **Materials:** *Mighty Minutes* 130, "Hello, How Are You?"; pictures of simple machines; chart paper
Read-Aloud	*My Neighbors and Their Simple Machines*	*My Neighbors and Their Simple Machines*
Small Group	**Option 1: Author Study** *Intentional Teaching Card* LL70, "Author Study"; several books by the same author and illustrator **Option 2: Simple Machines Author Study** *Intentional Teaching Card* LL70, "Author Study"; several books from the study by the same author and illustrator	**Option 1: Salsa** *Intentional Teaching Card* LL36, "Salsa"; ingredients; chart paper and marker; plastic knives; bowl **Option 2: Vegetable Soup** *Intentional Teaching Card* LL49, "Vegetable Soup"; chart paper and marker; plastic knives; cutting boards; colander
Mighty Minutes®	*Mighty Minutes* 154, "People Count"	*Mighty Minutes* 102, "Ten Wiggly Steps"

Make Time for…

Outdoor Experiences

- Review *Intentional Teaching Card* P41, "The Tortoise & the Hare." Follow the guidance on the card.

Family Partnerships

- Include families in the celebration by encouraging them and the children to explore the study displays and materials together.

Wow! Experiences

- Day 2: Celebration of the children's learning

Let's plan the celebration!

Vocabulary

English: *celebrate*

Spanish: *celebrar*

Question of the Day: What would you like to show our guests tomorrow at the celebration?

Large Group

Opening Routine:

- Sing a welcome song and talk about who's here.

Game: Sorting Syllables

- Use *Mighty Minutes* 95, "Sorting Syllables." Follow the guidance on the card using materials from the study.

Discussion and Shared Writing: Planning the Celebration

- Explain, "We have learned so much about simple machines. It's time to *celebrate* all of our hard work! When you celebrate, you do something special and fun. We will have our families and guests come visit to see everything that we have learned."

- Review the question of the day. Work together to create a plan to share the things that the children suggest. For example, you may say, "Gabby, you wanted to show the roller derby girl how you learned to take the nuts on and off the screws on the tire. I will write 'Set up tires and tools' on our plan." Document your plan on a sheet of chart paper.

- Once the plan has been made, discuss which parts of the plan each child would like to do and talk about what materials or supplies they may need.

English-Language Learners

Encourage families of English-language learners to visit the classroom so that the English-language learners, who might feel socially isolated, can talk with their families in their home languages. This will help children to continue to develop social and cognitive skills.

Before transitioning to interest areas, review each child's role in the plan and talk about how the children can help each other as they prepare for the celebration.

Choice Time

As you interact with children in the interest areas, make time to do the following:

- Support the children in setting up and gathering the materials for the celebration.

Read-Aloud

Read *My Neighbors and Their Simple Machines*. Pause repeatedly throughout the story and invite children to fill in the names of the machines and tools used.

Small Group

Option 1: Author Study

- Review *Intentional Teaching Card* LL70, "Author Study." Follow the guidance on the card.

Option 2: Author Study

- Review *Intentional Teaching Card* LL70, "Author Study." Follow the guidance on the card using an author whose books you have read during the study.

Mighty Minutes®

- Use *Mighty Minutes* 154, "People Count." Follow the guidance on the card.

Large-Group Roundup

- Recall the day's events.
- Review the plan you created at large-group time and talk about how the room is set up for the celebration.

Let's Celebrate!

Vocabulary

English: See *My Neighbors and Their Simple Machines* for words.
Question of the Day: What was your favorite part of the study?

Large Group

Opening Routine:

- Sing a welcome song and talk about who's here.

Song: "Hello, How Are You?"

- Use *Mighty Minutes* 130, "Hello, How Are You?" Follow the guidance on the card.

Discussion and Shared Writing: Sharing Simple Machines

- Welcome the families and guests to the classroom.

- Say, "We have learned so much about simple machines. What can we teach our guests about what we have learned?" Display a photo collection of simple machines for the children to refer to as they answer.

- Record their responses on a sheet of chart paper.

Before transitioning to interest areas, talk about the displays of children's learning that they've set up around the classroom.

Choice Time

As you interact with children in the interest areas, make time to do the following:

- Encourage the children to explain to the guests what they have learned about simple machines and share the displays that are set up around the classroom.

- Ask the children questions that encourage them to recall what they have learned.

- Assist the children and guests with using the different simple machines that are available.

Read-Aloud

Reread *My Neighbors and Their Simple Machines*. Encourage the children to retell the story for the guests.

Small Group

Option 1: Salsa

- Review *Intentional Teaching Card* LL36, "Salsa." Follow the guidance on the card.

- Talk with the children about the simple machines that they use to make the salsa.

Option 2: Vegetable Soup

- Review *Intentional Teaching Card* LL49, "Vegetable Soup." Follow the guidance on the card.

- Talk with the children about the simple machines that they use to make the soup.

Mighty Minutes®

- Use *Mighty Minutes* 102, "Ten Wiggly Steps." Follow the guidance on the card.

Large-Group Roundup

- Recall the day's events.

- Review the question of the day.

- Have the children help you create a thank-you note to the guests who attended the celebration. Post the note in the classroom for the families to see.

Reflecting on the Study

What were the most engaging parts of the study?

Are there other topics that might be worth investigating?

If I were to change any part of the study, what would it be?

Other thoughts and ideas:

Resources

Background Information for Teachers

Simple machines are devices that can be found in almost every area of the classroom and outdoors. There are many types of simple machines including inclined planes or ramps, screws, levers, pulleys, wedges, and wheels and axles. Some are small and handheld, such as scissors, lemon squeezers, and screws, while others are large, like loading ramps and flag pole pulleys. A *simple machine* is typically defined as "a device that changes the direction or magnitude of force." With this broad definition in mind, we can explore many different types of simple machines.

Studying simple machines offers children hands-on opportunities to experiment and explore their own ideas. They can compare what happens when you move a fulcrum of a lever from the middle to the end and discover how the threads of screws help hold things together. Children also have the opportunity to practice many social–emotional skills. For example, children will practice taking turns, cooperating, sharing ideas, and planning together as they make and modify simple machines. In a study of simple machines, you can guide children to learn how simple machines are used for all different types of tasks. As children explore these social–emotional, science, and social studies concepts, they will use skills in literacy, math, technology, and the arts.

Your knowledge of simple machines will help identify areas to focus on with children. Examine the simple machines in your community and consider the following questions as you plan for this new investigation.

- How have children shown interest in simple machines?

- How can simple machines reflect the diversity of your classroom?

- Which children in your room enjoy using different types of simple machines?

- How can you explore simple machines with children who have limited mobility?

- What simple machines do you already have in the classroom?

Think about the vocabulary you might use to talk about simple machines. While children may not learn and use all of these words, consider introducing them as you talk about simple machines.

angle: the space between two surfaces that meet each other

bolt: a metal rod with screw threads that is used to hold things together and is secured with a nut

cylinder: a three-dimensional shape made by connecting two identical circles with a curved plane

diameter: the width of a circle

effort: the force applied to a simple machine

force: physical strength or power

friction: the force that causes one thing to slow down as it rubs against something else

fulcrum: the support on which a lever moves

load: something that is carried or lifted

nut: a piece of metal with a hole in it that secures a bolt

rotate: to turn

screwdriver: a tool that is used to turn screws

slope: a slant

surface: the outside layer of something

tilt: a sloping surface

threads: the raised line that rotates around a screw or bolt

weight: how heavy something is

What do you want to research to help you understand this topic?

Children's Books

In addition to the children's books specifically used in this *Teaching Guide*, you may wish to supplement daily activities and interest areas with some of the listed children's books.

Additional books that accompany this *Teaching Guide*:

- *A Farmer's Life for Me* (Jan Dobbins)
  A farmer's life is very busy. There is always work to do! Follow this family and their friends as they spend their day working on the farm. As you read, invite the children to point out any simple machines the characters use such as levers or wheels and axles.

- *Lola Loves Stories* (Anna McQuinn)
  Lola is a little girl with a big imagination. She loves to read stories with her daddy every night, and the next day, she acts them out! After reading, invite the children to perform their own dramatic story retelling of a book they have read recently.

The following are **fiction** books about simple machines:

The Fort on Fourth Street: A Story About the Six Simple Machines (Lois Spangler) Told through cumulative rhyme similar to "The House that Jack Built," in this story a young girl named Kathleen builds a fort in her backyard with the help of Grandpa and the six simple machines. Follow the whole building process to discover the surprise reason the fort was built. After reading, invite children to build a fort with blocks or other materials and offer a few safe simple machines to help.

Tap Tap Bang Bang (Emma Garcia) All kinds of different tools are busy building a surprise in this colorful book packed with sound effects and action. Learn the names of construction tools and what they do, including unfamiliar ones like clamps, levels, and sanders. Invite children to make the sounds with you and model using the tools. As you read, ask children to predict what the tools are making.

And Everyone Shouted, "Pull!" A first look at forces in motion (Claire Llewellyn) Which simple machine will help the animals get their cart to the market? Wheels and axles of course! Follow the journey as they push and pull their way along. After you read, invite the children to fill their own cart and carry their own fruits and vegetables to the pretend market.

How Do You Lift a Lion? (Robert E. Wells) Take a look at how simple machines can help do all sorts of silly things like lift a lion or pull a panda. After you read, invite the children to think of other funny things that they could use simple machines to do.

Simple Machines: Wheels, Levers, and Pulleys (David A. Adler) Follow the cat to learn about how simple machines are used by children every day! As you read, invite the children to point out the simple machines they use at home, around their neighborhood, or at school.

Children's Books

Balancing Act (Ellen Stoll Walsh) How can the mice keep their teeter-totter balanced as more and more animals come along? Explore concepts of balance and compare and contrast the size of the animals as you read this story. After you read, invite the children to make their own lever and balance it using classroom materials.

Sam and Dave Dig A Hole (Mac Barnett) Sam and Dave want to find something spectacular, so they set off on a mission to dig a hole. What will they discover as they use their shovels to dig and dig and dig?

The Little Red Hen (Bonnie Dobkin) In this classic story of a hen whose friends aren't interested in helping her make the bread, there are several interesting tools used to prepare the flour for baking. As you read, invite children to keep a close eye out for simple machines. After reading, provide props and puppets for children to reenact the story.

Additional **Spanish-language or bilingual** books for this category include the following:

La Fortaleza de la calle cuatro: Una historia cerca de seis máquinas simples (Lois Spangler) Told through cumulative rhyme similar to "The House that Jack Built," in this story a young girl named Kathleen builds a fort in her backyard with the help of Grandpa and the six simple machines. Follow the whole building process to discover the surprise reason the fort was built. After reading, invite children to build a fort with blocks or other materials and offer a few safe simple machines to help.

Sam y Leo cavan un hoyo (Mac Barnettsian) Sam and Dave want to find something spectacular, so they set off on a mission to dig a hole. What will they discover as they use their shovels to dig and dig and dig?

La gallinita roja (Bonnie Dobkin) In this classic story of a hen whose friends aren't interested in helping her make the bread, there are several interesting tools used to prepare the flour for baking. As you read, invite children to keep a close eye out for simple machines. After reading, provide props and puppets for children to reenact the story.

The following books are **informational, nonfiction** books about simple machines:

Simple Machines (D.J. Ward) Brightly colored illustrations and simple text introduce the six simple machines and explain how they can be used together or on their own to make work easier. The book features bolded vocabulary, a glossary, and a prompt for a lever experiment. As you read, reinforce vocabulary words. Encourage children to identify simple machines they would find around the school and record their answers on a chart.

Simple Machines: Real Size Science (Rebecca Rissman) Real-size photographs accompany simple text to teach young readers about how simple machines look and function, from the massive construction crane to the humble egg beater. Concepts also include scale, proportion, and how machines are used. After reading, encourage children to discuss and compare the different simple machines. Ask, "How are levers different from screws? Can pulleys do the same work as a wedge?"

Children's Books

What is a Pulley? (Lloyd G. Douglas) Photographs and simple text featuring common pulleys like those on cranes and flagpoles introduce readers to the fundamental mechanics and structure of a pulley. Make a list of the pulleys featured in the book. Encourage children to think of other objects that might use pulleys and add them to the list.

What is a Wheel and Axle? (Lloyd G. Douglas) Full-color photographs and simple text featuring common wheels and axles like wheelbarrows and rolling pins introduce readers to the fundamental mechanics and structure of a wheel and axle. Ask, "What do wheels and axles allow objects to do?" Encourage each child to find a classroom toy or tool with a wheel and axle and demonstrate how it rolls.

How Toys Work: Ramps and Wedges (Sian Smith) Want to know how your half-pipe works? Labeled photographs and simple text help explain the scientific principles behind how ramps and wedges are used to make toys work. Ask children to find a partner and together either find a classroom toy that uses ramps or wedges or draw a toy that uses ramps or wedges. One child can explain whether the toy uses a ramp or a wedge, and the other child can show or explain how the toy works.

How Toys Work: Screws, Nuts, and Bolts (Sian Smith) Want to know how your robot works? Labeled photographs and simple text help explain the scientific principles behind how screws, nuts, and bolts are used to make toys work. After reading, offer children nuts and bolts to explore. Encourage children to notice how the nuts and bolts work together. Ask children, "How are bolts and screws different? Can you find any classroom toys with screws or bolts in them?"

Going Ice Fishing: Lever vs. Screw (Mari Schuh) A group of children want to go ice fishing, but they will have to move some of the ice on a lake before they can get started. They compare two simple machines, the lever and the screw, and decide which one would do a better job of moving the ice. Before reading, explain that the children in the book will have to decide whether to use a lever or a screw to move ice off a lake. Ask children to predict what the group will decide and explain why. After reading, ask children if they can think of any other simple machines the group could have used.

Hauling a Pumpkin: Wheels and Axles vs. Lever (Mari Schuh) A group of children have picked out their pumpkins from the pumpkin patch, but now they need to haul them away. They compare two simple machines, the lever and the wheels and axles, and decide which one would do a better job of moving the pumpkins. Before reading, ask children to predict which machine the group will decide to use. After reading, invite children to try moving sturdy cushions or heavy beanbags with a lever or wheels and axles. Encourage children to share their observations.

Mr. Ferris and His Wheel (Kathryn Gibbs Davis) America is hosting the 1893 World's Fair, and the organizers need something amazing, something original and inspiring, to compete with the last fair's marvel in Paris, the Eiffel Tower. This biography tells the story of how George Ferris stepped up with a vision of an enormous wheel and axle and overcame the odds to make his dream a reality. This brightly colored book may need to be read in two sessions. Ask children to share their experiences with Ferris wheels. Invite children to design and draw a new amusement park ride based on simple machines.

Children's Books

Incredible Inventions (Lee Bennett Hopkins) Inventions come in all shapes and sizes, from roller coasters to crayons, basketball to Band-Aids®, but they all start with someone's creative idea and a little imagination. This collection of sixteen original poems celebrates amazing inventions. Encourage children to write or recite poems about something they would like to invent. Help children learn more about inventions and the inventing process from videos and articles online. See *Intentional Teaching Card* LL26, "Searching the Web," for information about searching the Internet with children.

Additional **Spanish-language or bilingual** books for this category include the following:

Como funcionan las palancas / How Levers Work (Jim Mezzanotte) This photo book with simple text helps explain the scientific principles behind levers. After reading, offer children materials to construct and experiment moving objects using levers. Take photos or videos as children work to document their actions and language.

Como funcionan las rampas, las cunas, y los tornillos / How Ramps, Wedges and Screws Work (Jim Mezzanotte) This photo book with simple text helps explain the scientific principles behind ramps, wedges, and screws. After reading, invite children identify and label ramps, wedges, and screws in and around the classroom using sticky notes of different colors. Support them to write the words *ramp, wedge,* and *screw* on the sticky notes.

Como funcionan las ruedas y los ejes / How Weels and Axles Work (Jim Mezzanotte) This photo book with simple text helps explain the scientific principles behind wheels and axles. After reading, encourage children to use recycled materials to construct and experiment using wheels and axles. Encourage children to make observational drawings of their constructions.

Utilizo máquinas simples (Buffy Silverman) This bright photo book shows where simple machines are found—everywhere! Photos show everyday items and point out the simple machines within. After reading, invite children to gather similar simple machines around the classroom and illustrate pictures explaining how they help us work.

What Do Wheels Do All Day? / ¿Qué hacen las ruedas todo el día (April Jones Prince) This concept book on the wheel illustrates the wide variety of wheels—bike wheels, car tires, wooden wheels, pinwheels—and demonstrates the many different ways people use wheels to go. Use this book to introduce wheels and how people *roll* and *turn* them in simple and complex machines. Invite children to use photos and magazine pictures to make a collage of different wheels and people using wheels.

Children's Books

The following books feature **people who work with simple machines**:

Tools (Taro Miura) Who do you think of when you see a hammer, a saw, and some nails? Spreads of labeled simple tools in this nearly wordless book prompt readers to guess which professional uses each set before they turn the page and see the tools in use. As you read, pause to allow children to guess. Use this book to talk about how simple machines can be used and combined in a variety of ways for different jobs. Invite children to choose a job and draw or collect the tools they need to do it.

Chop, Simmer, Season (Alexa Brandenberg) Discover how simple machines are used in the kitchen as these two chefs prepare a feast for their hungry friends. As you read, invite the children to point out the simple machines they notice and talk about how the chefs are using them. After reading, set up a cooking activity for the children to participate in that incorporates simple machines.

Whose Tools are These? (Sharon Katz Cooper) Who uses scissors and a blow dryer? Who uses a screwdriver? Who uses a knife? Take a look inside this engaging picture book to discover who works with different kinds of simple machines and other tools.

I Want to be a Chef (Dan Liebman) Go behind the scenes at a restaurant and learn what it takes to be a chef as you see every aspect of a chef's job. From training to proper food handling, this book shows you what goes into being a successful restaurant chef. As you read, look at the pictures and point out simple machines that chefs use such as kitchen knives and forks.

Whose Tools? (Toni Buzzeo, Tim Datz) This illustrated picture book shows you the tools that six different craftsmen and women use. Point out simple machines such as a chisel, snips, and pliers as you discover the tools of their trades.

Girls Think of Everything: Stories of Ingenious Inventions by Women (Catherine Thimmesh and Melissa Sweet) Have you ever wondered who invented the ice cream cone, the fire escape, or a fruit press? This book tells you all about the women who made these useful inventions along with many more. Choose one or two stories to share with children at a time. As you read about their inventions, point out any simple machines that are used. After reading, provide paper and scrap materials in the Art area for the children to use to create their own inventions.

A Day in the Life of a Builder (Linda Hayward) A builder named Jack is working on building five new homes. This book shows you what it takes to be a builder. It shows you the process a builder goes through to build a house that the family will love and the tools that they use.

Delivery (Anastasia Suen) From letters and packages to newspapers, there are so many types of things that are delivered each day. Discover how things are delivered and who delivers them in this illustrated picture book. As you read, encourage the children to notice how simple machines make delivering things easier for workers.

Additional **Spanish-language or bilingual** books for this category include the following:

Corta y para: Un libro sobre cuñas (Michael Dahl) A lumberjack carrying an ax is featured in this book demonstrating how wedges are used. As you read, encourage

Children's Books

children to think of other ways big jobs like cutting down trees might be accomplished without simple machines.

In Christina's Toolbox / En la caja de herramientas de Cristina (Dianne Homan) Christina, whose mother is a carpenter, loves to use the tools in her toolbox to make repairs around the house. After reading, invite children to describe their experiences using tools. Encourage children to experiment using simple tools.

¡Pégale! Historia de las herramientas (Dona Rice) This fascinating book explains how the tools we use today were first created and how they have changed over time. As you read, invite children to describe how these tools are used and who uses them. After reading, encourage children to experiment creating their own tools using the materials they have in the classroom. You might ask questions like, "Can you make a tool out of these craft sticks?"

Obrero de Construcción (Heather Miller) See how construction workers use manual and power tools to build. As you read, encourage children to notice how simple machines help carpenters and construction workers build.

The following are **alphabet and numbers** books:

ABCs at the Park (Rebecca Rissman) This book takes you on a trip around the park to find everyday items that begin with each letter of the alphabet. As you look at the illustrations with the children, point out simple machines such as inclined planes and screws.

Dig! (Andrea Zimmerman) See how Mr. Rally uses complex machines and simple machines as he counts through all of the digging jobs that he has to do. Invite children to name the tools and machinery they see throughout the book.

Counting Tools 1 to 10 (Rebecca Bonde) Explore counting through this bright picture book that features simple machines such as hammers and screwdrivers, along with other hand tools. Invite the children to count the tools on each page as you share this story.

Dining with… Monsters!: A Disgusting Way to Count to 10! (Agnese Baruzzi) Grab your forks and knives, it's time to ear with some monsters! Discover what disgusting things monsters like as you count through their meals.

Alphabet Under Construction (Denise Fleming) Follow the mouse as he constructs each letter of the alphabet in this busy picture book. As you read with the children, challenge them to point out any simple machines that the mouse uses to make his letters. After reading, display this book in the Art area and invite the children to use the art and woodworking materials to make their own alphabet.

The Numberlys (William Joyce) This book takes you back to a time when there were only numbers, no letters at all. This was until a group of five heroes decided that they needed more. They got to work and used their tools to start breaking apart numbers to create letters. After much hard work, they had done it! They created all 26 letters of the alphabet. As you read, talk with the children about the numbers and letters they recognize.

Children's Books

The Alphabet Book (P.D. Eastman) This silly picture book takes you through each letter of the alphabet showing you a silly object that goes with each letter along the way. See what simple machines you can find throughout the book!

Additional **Spanish-language or bilingual** books for this category include the following:

Números y Palabritas y otras locuras loquitas (Luis Darmo Bernal) This colorful book is full of silly stories about numbers and counting. As you read, talk with the children about the numbers they recognize and the words they hear.

Albertina anda arriba: el abecedario / Albertina Goes Up: An Alphabet Book (Nancy Maria Grande Tabor) A group of silly animals go exploring through the Spanish alphabet. On each page, invite children to join you in naming and sounding out letters. After reading, invite children to create their own alphabet book featuring simple machines.

ABeCedario musical (Yanitizia Canetti) This photo book features children playing musical instruments from A to Z set to a rhyming chant. As you read, invite children to look carefully at the instruments. You might ask, "Do you see any simple machines here?" as you show instruments' keys or tuning pegs.

The following books focus on **families, feelings, and friendship**:

Chicken Chickens (Valeri Gorbachev) When two little chickens go to the playground for the very first time, everything seems so big and new that they are afraid to try anything with the other kids. They work up the courage to try the slide, but freeze at the top. Fortunately, a new friend helps them overcome their fear and have fun. Ask children to share their experiences with trying challenging new things. Invite children to talk about how friends can help each other when they're scared.

Where's the Ramp? (Lisa Andrea McCarthy) Linda's cousin Roy depends on a wheelchair, but when he comes to visit and the family decides to go out for dinner, they find that restaurants with entry ramps are surprisingly scarce. As the family searches all over for an accessible restaurant to enjoy their evening, they start to fear it may be a hopeless case. Use the book to start a conversation about how access to ramps help people do the things they want and need to do. Ask the children how they would feel if they could not get to where they wanted to go.

The Night Worker (Kate Banks) Alex's dad works on a construction site at night. Alex misses his dad when he is at work and wants to go with him. One night, Alex's dad has a special surprise for him, his very own hard hat! Alex finally gets to spend the night with his dad at the construction site. Encourage the children to talk about how they think Alex feels when he gets to visit the construction site with his dad.

Children's Books

Drew the Screw (Mattia Cerato) All of the other tools are helping the boy build a treehouse, and Drew the screw wants to help, too. However, he doesn't know what his job is, and because he hasn't been used, he worries that he can't do cool things like the other tools. But when the boy does come for him, Drew's job turns out to be perfect for him. Ask children to identify the simple machines in the story. Invite children to share their experiences with wanting to help someone.

The Little Snowplow (Lora Koehler) On the Mighty Mountain Road Crew, all the trucks are big, except for the new little snowplow. The other trucks don't think he can handle the big storms, but the little snowplow knows he can, and he trains to be ready when the big snowstorm finally arrives. Encourage children to share their experiences with practicing for a big event. Ask, "How do you think the little snowplow felt when he worked in the blizzard?"

The Most Magnificent Thing (Ashley Spires) A creative young girl decides she is going to make the most magnificent thing ever. She thinks it will be easy because she makes things all the time, but instead she fails over and over, until she gets so angry she quits. Her best canine friend convinces her to take a walk and cool down, and when she returns she manages to make the magnificent thing just right. Invite children to share their experiences with trying challenging things. Ask, "How does it feel when you can't get something just right? How do you feel better?"

Big Ernie's New Home: A Story for Young Children Who Are Moving (Teresa Martin) Big Ernie is moving to a new home, and at first he feels sad, upset, and anxious about leaving his familiar community and usual routines. Gradually, however, he discovers the same comforts he always loved and exciting adventures in his new home, and soon he starts to feel better. Use this book to help children who have just moved to the school feel comfortable with their feelings or to prepare children for welcoming or saying good-bye to a classmate. Ask, "What about his new home made Ernie feel unhappy? What new things made him happy?"

Building Our House (Jonathan Bean) A girl and her family pack up their house in the city and work together to build a new home from the ground up in the country. The girl and her brother help Mom and Dad through every stage of the building process, from empty lot to finished home, and get their hands dirty with machines, vehicles, and all kinds of house-making jobs. Imagined from the eyes of his older sister, the author retells his family's true experience and provides photographs in the afterword. Invite children to share a story about a time they helped their family with a big project. Ask, "What do you like best about your home? What makes it special to you?"

Children's Books

Additional **Spanish-language or bilingual** books for this category include the following:

Salsa: Un Poema Para Cocinar (Jorge Argueta) In this poem, a young boy and his sister sing and dance as they gather the ingredients for salsa and grind them up in a molcajete, a special tool their ancestors used. When they finish chopping and mixing, their whole family fetches tortillas and plates and dances salsa in anticipation. Encourage children to talk about cooking with their families and any special tools they use. Ask, "What special foods do you eat at home? How do you feel when you eat them?" If children are interested in making salsa, you may follow the book's recipe or see *Intentional Teaching Card* LL36, "Salsa," for help.

Platón El Ornitorrinco Plomero (de medio tiempo) / Plato the Platypus Plumber (part-time) (Hazel Edwards, John Petropoulos) Plato the Platypus is a plumber who fixes pipes, but that's not all he does! Plato also helps grumpy people feel better using humor and his magic smile spray. Follow his adventures as he helps the community and his friend Zanzibar's family. After reading ask the children, "What can you do to help someone feel better?" and "Has a friend ever helped you?"

Construyendo (Sally Sutton and Brian Lovelock) This colorful board book illustrates how machines of all kinds are used in construction. Encourage children to notice how construction workers work together to use simple machines.

The following books feature **make-believe and imagination**:

Queen Victoria's Bathing Machine (Gloria Whelan) It is so very hot out this summer, and Queen Victoria of England would love to cool off with a swim in the ocean. But, as the queen of a country, it would be improper and embarrassing for her royal subjects to see in her bathing suit. It's up to her husband, Prince Albert, to invent a "bathing machine" to let her swim sight unseen. Use the book to start a discussion about how people invent new things to solve problems. Invite children to think of a problem they would like to solve with an invention and encourage them to draw their design for the machine.

Chen Ping and His Magic Axe (Demi) Chen Ping works hard for a rich and greedy master, and one day on his way to chop wood he accidentally drops his axe in the river. When a helpful stranger offers him a silver axe and a golden axe, honest Chen Ping accepts only his plain axe, and the stranger rewards him by enchanting the plain axe with a useful spell. The greedy man throws his axe in the river to get an enchanted axe, too, but his selfishness costs him. Offer children props and costumes and invite them to retell or reenact the story. Record the story on video for children to watch later.

The Adventures of Beekle: The Unimaginary Friend (Dan Santat) Beekle waits and waits in the world of imagination for a real child to imagine him, but it never happens. He decides to take matters into his own hands and travel to the real world to find his perfect match. Follow Beekle on his magical journey along the way.

Children's Books

Cooking With Henry and Elliebelly (Carolyn Parkhurst) Henry and his little sister Elliebelly have a make-believe cooking show, and today they're making waffles. They disagree on a lot of things—Henry says they need to dress like chefs, and Elliebelly insists on pirate hats—but they persist through minor spats and complications to mix up their pretend ingredients and enjoy Mom's real waffles. Encourage children to talk about games they play with their siblings. Ask, "How do you feel when someone you're playing with has different ideas from you? How do you work things out?"

How to Dig a Hole to the Other Side of the World (Faith McNulty) Follow a child's imaginary journey as he uses simple machines to dig and drill his way to the center of the earth. As you read, invite the children to point out the different kinds of simple machines the child uses and talk about what they do.

The Unhappy Stonecutter: A Japanese Folk Tale (Charlotte Guillain) This book tells the tale of an unhappy stonecutter. Follow his journey as he discovers how to be happy with what he has. As you read, ask the children to notice what tools and simple machines he uses to cut the stones.

Additional **Spanish-language or bilingual** books for this category include the following:

Como cavar un hoyo hasta el otro lado del mundo (Faith McNulty) Follow a child's imaginary journey as he uses simple machines to dig and drill his way to the center of the earth. As you read, invite the children to point out the different kinds of simple machines the child uses and talk about what they do.

Carlos Digs to China / Carlos excava hasta el China (Jan Romero Stevens) Carlos loves Chinese food so much he decides to dig a tunnel to China to find the best Chinese food. After reading, encourage children to describe the simple machines that Carlos should use to dig such a deep tunnel.

El robot desordenado (Greg Roza) What happens when a robot makes a mess? Invite children to draw a robot made up of simple machines. As children draw, encourage them to describe how the robot will move and how it will work.

Teacher Resources

The teacher resources provide you with additional information and ideas for enhancing and extending the study topic.

Experiments with Simple Machines (Salvatore Tocci) This book shares a variety of different experiments to do with the children along with useful resources and a list of important words and their meanings.

Simple Machines Made Simple (Ralph E. St. Andre) This book looks at each types of simple machines and provides information in an easy to share way. Through experiments and examples of everyday objects, this book will help the reader better understand simple machines and how they work.

Explore Simple Machines!: With 25 Great Projects (Anita Yasuda) This book offers a collection of interesting engineering projects to do with children. Explore these hands-on simple machines activities.

Weekly Planning Form

Week of: _______________________   Teacher: _______________________   Study: _______________________

	Monday	Tuesday	Wednesday	Thursday	Friday
Interest Areas					
Large Group					
Read-Aloud					
Small Group					

Outdoor Experiences:

Family Partnerships:

Wow! Experiences:

©2016 Teaching Strategies, LLC, Bethesda, MD; www.TeachingStrategies.com
Permission is granted to duplicate the material on this page for use in programs implementing *The Creative Curriculum® for Preschool*.

Weekly Planning Form, continued

Reflecting on the week:

"To Do" List:

Individual Child Planning

©2016 Teaching Strategies, LLC, Bethesda, MD; www.TeachingStrategies.com
Permission is granted to duplicate the material on this page for use in programs implementing *The Creative Curriculum® for Preschool*.